BOOKSHELF

MAKING IT MANUFACTURING TECHNIQUES

L'A

TASCHEN

siècle

Karl Schaberg
Manfred
Schenkenberg
Christiane Fricke
Klaus Honnef
Edie P. Wacker
Inge P. Wacker

HOW
ART!
The London Design Festival 15-25 September 2007

the jou
the thin
t of
home-work
f the
Royal College of Ar
20 April 199
supported by
Leonard Cheshire

Minimalismo
Minimalism

SISIS Ed. Uta Grosenick

TASCHEN

BOOKSHELF
Alex Johnson

305 color illustrations

Thames & Hudson

For my father and mother,
   who gave me my first bookshelves
For Wilma,
   who shares my bookshelves
And for Thomas, Edward and Robert,
   who are rapidly filling up their own bookshelves

On the cover: Archive (page 214),
Upside Down (page 90, photo
by Aurélien Mole), Hô (page 20),
Puckman (page 69), Laderszat (page 52);
On page 1: Falling Bookend (page 269);
On pages 2–3: Between the Lines (page 242).

First published in 2012 in hardcover in the
United States of America by Thames & Hudson Inc.,
500 Fifth Avenue, New York, New York 10110

thamesandhudsonusa.com

Library of Congress Catalog Card Number 2011935784

ISBN 978-0-500-51614-0

Printed and bound in China by Everbest Printing Co. Ltd

> ❝ **A multitude of books confuses the mind. Accordingly, since you cannot read all the books which you may possess, it is enough to possess only as many books as you can read.** ❞
>
> Seneca, *Letters to Lucilius*

Aakkoset >
Material Abachi hardwood
Dimensions 170 × 40 × 185 cm/
66⅞ × 15¾ × 72⅞ in.
||||||||||||||||||||||||||||||||||||||||||||||||||||||||||||||||||||||||||||||||||||
Intended to function as both bookcase and room divider,
the alphabetical Aakkoset weighs a hefty 300 kg (660 lbs).
Helsinki-based designer Lincoln Kayiwa was born in Uganda,
and has selected a tropical African tree as the raw material
for his shelf.
www.kayiwa.fi

Dimensions are given in the form width × depth × height,
unless otherwise stated.

Contents

A Medley
of Bookcases

1/

A Cornucopia of Designs

114

2/

Introduction
In Praise of the Bookshelf

> **Up, and to my chamber doing several things there of moment,
> and then comes Sympson, the Joyner; and he and I with great pains
> contriving presses to put my books up in: they now growing numerous,
> and lying one upon another on my chairs …**
>
> **Samuel Pepys, 23 July 1666**

Over the last 20 years we have experienced
a revolution in the way we store our knowledge.
Yet while we can now shrink an entire personal library
to an electronic device the size and weight of a single
paperback, there has also been an explosion in the
creativity behind the design of that most basic
household item, the bookshelf.

Bookshelves today are no longer just somewhere
to store books. They are modern art, engineering
experiments and – just as they were for Samuel Pepys
350 years ago – status symbols. Despite the rapid rise
of e-readers, the bookshelf continues to play an active
role in 21st-century culture, whether appearing in
the dubious expense claims of British Members of

Parliament, or on Sydney's Bondi Beach, where in 2009
Ikea installed 30 of its bestselling Billy bookcases to
celebrate the design's 30th birthday. Financial analysts
at Bloomberg have used sales of the Billy as an index
of economic growth. Bookshelves even managed
to steal the show at the Victoria & Albert Museum's
'Architects Build Small Spaces' exhibition in 2010.
The Ark book tower – a mildly swaying, free-standing
wooden tower by Rintala Eggertsson Architects from
Norway – was built from hundreds of filled
bookshelves into which readers could climb,
and sit and read.

Henry Petroski, author of the definitive history
The Book on the Bookshelf (1999), argues that the

standard bookcase shape in England was approaching the design with which we are now familiar by the 16th century. Before that, books were usually kept in chests: small, reasonably portable boxes owned by the wealthier members of society (see Bijou Bookshelves, pages 244–67, for modern takes on these). But even in the early history of the bookcase there were plenty of intriguing concepts, such as Italian military engineer Agostino Ramelli's 1588 revolving bookwheel. His design, resembling a waterwheel, was mounted on an axle with shelves that would counter-rotate as the whole turned. His drawings showed how a mechanism adapted from astronomical clocks could ensure that the books and shelves remained at a secure 45-degree angle to the floor. It was never built; Ramelli was simply exhibiting his ingenuity and engineering skills. However, Justin Pollard, in his 2010 book *Boffinology: The Real Stories*

Behind Our Greatest Scientific Discoveries, suggests that the idea of the bookwheel (a device that allowed the user to flick between pages of information) was a forerunner of the Internet.

Over 400 years after Ramelli's design, the new architects of our home libraries have injected a similar *joie de vivre* into bookshelf design. Shelves have now become ingenious 'theatres' in which our books parade, rather than collections of planks for storage. Take, for example, the Bibliochaise chair (page 147) designed by Italian company Nobody&co; a comfortable leather armchair, it also holds 5 metres (16 ft) of books. According to designer Alisée Matta, the inspiration came from living in a small apartment filled with books, but with nowhere to sit. 'Sitting and living in the middle of your favourite books is a very strong feeling,' she says, 'like sitting in the middle of yourself, of your mind – every book you read becomes part of you and of who you are.'

William Gladstone, 19th-century British Premier, would probably not have enjoyed the recent innovations. 'It has been a fashion to make bookcases highly ornamental,' he wrote disapprovingly in his 1890 article 'On Books and the Housing of Them', arguing that books require no ornament and that they must be fixed, preferably against a wall. I suspect he would not have been too keen on Arunkumar Francis's shelf Study on Sensational Designs either (overleaf).

Bibliochaise (page 147)

||||||||||||||||||||||||||||||||||||||||||||||||||||||||||||||||||||||||||||||||||||||||

There is no requirement for books to be shelved in rectangular units on walls. Many of the most exciting new designs incorporate shelves into everyday items of furniture such as lamps, tables and chairs.

Study on Sensational Designs
Unbuilt study

||||||||||||||||||||||||||||||||||||||||||||||||||||||||||||||||||||||||||||||||||||||||||||||

Bookshelves can be playful as well as useful, revealing the personality of their owner just as much as the books that they hold.

http://arun-francis.blogspot.com

'Design outcome can be sensible, sensual, sentimental, senseless or downright sensational,' says Francis. 'To design a shelf was the focus here, a single line flowing through the shelf to make out an expression, a shelf that makes the observer go "wow" , in this case plain "sexy".'

But is this new renaissance in bookcase design a last hurrah before books vanish into computers (as music has done), to be conjured up at the push of a button? Or rather might the increasingly impressive sales of e-books herald a new chapter in home decoration? With fewer books to be housed, perhaps readers will look for more exciting ways of storing their home libraries than a mere shelf, with the bookcase becoming closer to a trophy cabinet. The determination to save the book may also see people move towards treasuring their volumes in fitting surroundings. Indeed, special-edition furniture is now being sold in galleries that were once the domain of the artist. Some designers – such as Ron Arad, designer of the serpentine Bookworm, and Peter Marigold (whose Sum bookshelves appear opposite and on page 29) –

are already selling limited editions of their shelving this way.

Although e-books are seen as a convenient alternative, the desire to own printed books remains strong for many, even among younger readers. In an interview with the *Wall Street Journal*, Penguin Group CEO John Makinson made the distinction between the 'book reader' (who is as happy to read digital books as paper ones) and the 'book owner', who 'wants to give, share and shelve books. They love the experience.' It's an experience that writer Nathan Schneider believes is central to his existence. In his 2010 article 'The New Memory Theater', Schneider's

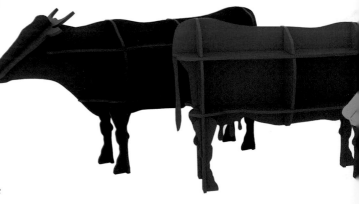

Sum (page 29)

||||||||||||||||||||||||||||||||||||||||||||||||||||||||||||||||||||||||||||||||||||||||||||||||||||||||

Rather than being unobtrusive and overlooked, bookshelves are now becoming elements of interior decor that deliberately attract the gaze and demand to be investigated.

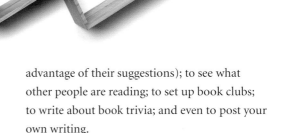

concern is chiefly for what might happen if bookshelves disappear. Schneider regards his shelves as extensions of his body, and finds simply browsing them stimulates his mind and brings back memories.

There is, of course, no reason why physical and virtual bookshelves cannot be complementary. Literary social-networking sites such as Goodreads (www.goodreads.com) and LibraryThing (www.librarything.com) are thriving – Goodreads alone has over five million members worldwide. As well as providing an online way of cataloguing your collection, the websites offer a number of other benefits, including the chance to recommend titles to like-minded readers (and take

advantage of their suggestions); to see what other people are reading; to set up book clubs; to write about book trivia; and even to post your own writing.

What online bookcases cannot provide is that sense of public display, offering visible pointers to guests and clients as to who you are (or would like to be perceived to be). Your bookcase design says (almost) as much about you as the books on show.

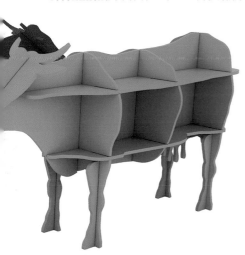

Estante Vaco

Materials Wood
Dimensions Various

||||||||||||||||||||||||||||||||||||||||||||||||||||||||||||||||||||||||||||||||||||||||||||||||||||||||

Designer Dennys Tormen won first prize in the inaugural Brazilian Sustainable Design Competition with this cow-shaped bookcase: all materials were sourced from a cooperative that turns waste paper into a plate-like substance.

www.dennystormen.com

Central library, Hjørring, Denmark

Materials Linoleum, MDF, epoxy floor, textiles, foam
Dimensions 4,900 m²/
52,700 ft²
||||||||||||||||||||||||||||||||||||||||||||||||||||||||||||||||||||||||||||||||||||||||||||||||||||||||||
The bookshelf acts as a serpentine spine to the central library,
redesigned by Rune Fjord in cooperation with Rosan Bosch.
They describe it as 'a sort of meeting place that encourages
engagement as well as active participation'.
www.runefjord.dk
www.rosanbosch.com

When Michelle Obama was photographed with
Samantha Cameron at 10 Downing Street during
the 2011 presidential visit to London, not only
did the media put considerable detective work into
deciphering the titles on the Camerons' bookshelves,
but they also went to pains to work out what model
of bookcase they were resting on.

A radical overhaul of bookshelf design might
even help to save libraries – an increasingly
endangered species in many countries as a result
of government spending cuts. Rune Fjord and Rosan
Bosch completely redesigned the interior of the
central library in Hjørring, Denmark, to feature
a central snaking structure that winds through the
library, changing function as it turns from bookshelf
to table to counter and back to bookshelf again. It is
a striking decoration in itself, but the designers also
believe that the shelf points, guides and tempts
visitors to explore the library area.

The truth for many readers is that their
bookshelves are nearly as important to them as their
books. I remember the size and shape and smell of
my childhood bookcases with as much fondness as
I recall the Mumfie, Jennings, Tintin and pocket-sized
Observer's guides that sat on them. What bookcases
and bookshelves provide – whether they are shaped
like polar bears, made of felt or hold books upside
down (all of which can be found in the following
pages) – is a welcoming habitat. Alberto Manguel's
portrayal of reading at home in *The Library at Night*
(2006) is one of the most evocative descriptions
of how a collection of books becomes more than a
pile of papers, how even the very smell of his wooden
shelves relaxes him. This is the library as emotional
sanctuary. A survey of 4,000 people by UK insurers

Legal & General ('The Changing Face of British Homes', 2008) suggests that many really do value this kind of space. When asked which feature room they would most like to have in their new home, 15 per cent said they wanted a library, compared to 13 per cent who chose a gym, 9 per cent a music studio and 8 per cent a home cinema.

This sanctuary does not need to be as substantial as a grand room full of books. Individual objects such as the plywood Isokon Penguin Donkey (designed by Egon Riss and Jack Pritchard in the 1930s) can be much-loved items associated with, and conducive to, reading. Playwright Tom Stoppard has spoken about the pleasure that his Book Satchel (by Manhattan-based luggage designer T. Anthony) has given him over several decades. Now out of production, the satchel is a case made of leather, steel and wood that holds a selection of books in style, yet is small enough to be carried as hand-luggage. 'It's like bringing a bit of home with you,' he told the *New York Times*.

Readers like to give good homes to their favourite books: playing with, arranging and rearranging them. As a child, I loved my *Nutshell Library* by Maurice Sendak, a boxed, four-volume set that included

WaSnake
Materials LEDs, optical fibres, wood, elastomer
Dimensions Various

||||||||||||||||||||||||||||||||||||||||||||||||||||||||||||||||||||||||||||||||||||||||||||||||||

Designers are embracing new technology to produce bookshelves that can do far more than simply store books in parallel lines: the WaSnake display news from chosen RSS feeds and even SMS messages.
www.nodesign.net

an alphabet book, *Chicken Soup with Rice* (a book of rhymes about each month), a counting book and a cautionary tale. I enjoyed reading the books themselves, but also took pleasure in simply taking the volumes out and replacing them in their proper places. Now a little older, I have enjoyed sharing them with my young children, and, in the intervening period, have developed a slightly costly grownup delight in the Folio Society's slipcases.

In 1901, John Willis Clark wrote about the 'ever-present need for more space to hold the invading hordes of books that represent the literature of today' in his fascinating and groundbreaking study of library fixtures and fittings, *The Care of Books*. Over a century later we are still faced with the same, happy, problem. The bookshelf is in rude health.

part 1/

A Medley of
Bookcases

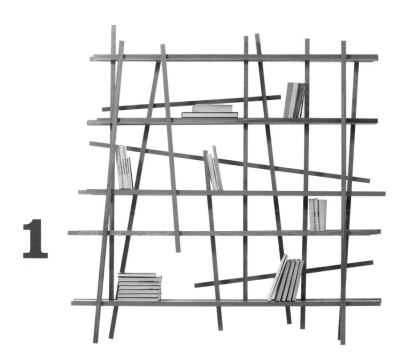

1

To what degree can you redesign a box? Although the traditional shape of the bookshelf has remained relatively unchanged over the last several centuries, designers in recent years have discovered potential for evolution within the confines of the essentially rectangular, fixed-shelf structure. There has been relatively little research done into the aesthetics of bookshelf design itself, but one tantalizing suggestion is that a correlation exists between the fourth shelf of Ikea's Billy bookcase and the golden ratio used in art, architecture and book design. Interdisciplinary artist John D. Freyer and social anthropologist Johan Lindquist believe this is the shelf where 'the vast majority display books that most clearly illustrate their identity aspirations'.

One of the joys of curating the design blog that inspired this book is seeing how bookshelf design is flourishing. On an almost daily basis, designers and fans from all over the world post photographs of new and intriguing bookshelves. Inevitably there are criticisms from visitors to the site – that the bookcases hold very few books (a claim that is often untrue), or that the unusual designs could damage books (again, usually not the case). The vast majority of comments simply express wonder at the creativity and welcome the continuing breath of fresh air into an area of design that is ripe for renewal. One of the most common queries is 'Where can I buy this?'

Home

Material Lacquered MDF

Dimensions 170 × 29 × 180 cm/
66⅞ × 11½ × 70⅞ in.

||||||||||||||||||||||||||||||||||||||||||||||||||||||||||||||||||||||

The various modules of Harry Allen's
design can be placed together to build
and rebuild an ideal home (including
attic, stairs, lawn, garage and garden)
for your books.

www.harryallendesign.com

Library
Materials Ash, powder-coated steel
Dimensions Various
|||||||||||||||||||||||||||||||||||||||||||||||||||||||||||||||||||||||||||||||||||||||||||||||||||||||||||||||||||||||
This bookcase was designed by Thomas Bentzen with office spaces and reception areas in mind, but has a welcomingly domestic – almost childlike – feel to it too. Three sizes are available, and books and magazines may also be stored on the roofs.
www.thomasbentzen.com

Hô

Material Lacquered beech

Dimensions 64 × 50 × 240 cm/
25¼ × 19¾ × 94½ in.

||||||||||||||||||||||||||||||||||||||||||||||||||||||||||||||||||||||||||||||||||||||||||||||

A ladder that can also be used as a bookcase, or a bookcase that also be used as a ladder? This design by Jocelyn Deris can hold up to a hundred books, none of which will be out of reach.

www.jocelynderis.com

Kantik

Material Powder-coated MDF

Dimensions 110 × 110 × 190 cm/
43⅝ × 43⅝ × 74⅞ in.

||||||||||||||||||||||||||||||||||||||||||||||||||||||||||||||||||||||||||

Kantik is a single, solid board, designed
to lean against the wall. Books are held
in place by their own weight, and the
cut-out sections provide space for
volumes of various sizes. Designed
by Patricia Yasmine Graf for the
Freundliche Übernahme (friendly
takeover) online design store.

www.pyg-design.de

Slip Shelf

Material Sprayed MDF

Dimensions 50 × 50 × 200 cm/
63 × 63 × 78¾ in.

||||||||||||||||||||||||||||||||||||||||||||||||||||||||||||||||||||||||

Gitta Gschwendtner's bookcase appears
to be slipping down the wall under
the weight of the books it holds.
At the bottom, the upturned shelves
form a useful magazine rack.

www.gittagschwendtner.com

Of Wars & Wits & Power

Materials Wood, powder-coated steel, gold-plated
die-cast aluminium
Dimensions 110 × 50 × 180 cm/
43⅜ × 19¾ × 70⅞ in.

||||||||||||||||||||||||||||||||||||||||||||||||||||||||||||||||||||||||||||||||||||

A bookcase that depicts the continuing efforts of countries
to protect their land with missile systems. The golden army,
strategically placed underneath, upholds and protects their plans.
www.coroflot.com/daniellove

Libri
Material Lacquered ash
Dimensions 38 × 29 × 280 cm/
14¾ × 11½ × 110 in.
||||||||||||||||||||||||||||||||||||||||||||||||||||||||||||||||||||||
A minimalist, ladder-like approach to
shelving, Libri by Michaël Bihain stands
against the wall to form a solid rack.
Alternatively, the units can be used in
a series, or stand against one other to
form a pyramid. Bihain also created
the Patatras bookshelf on page 226.
www.bihain.com

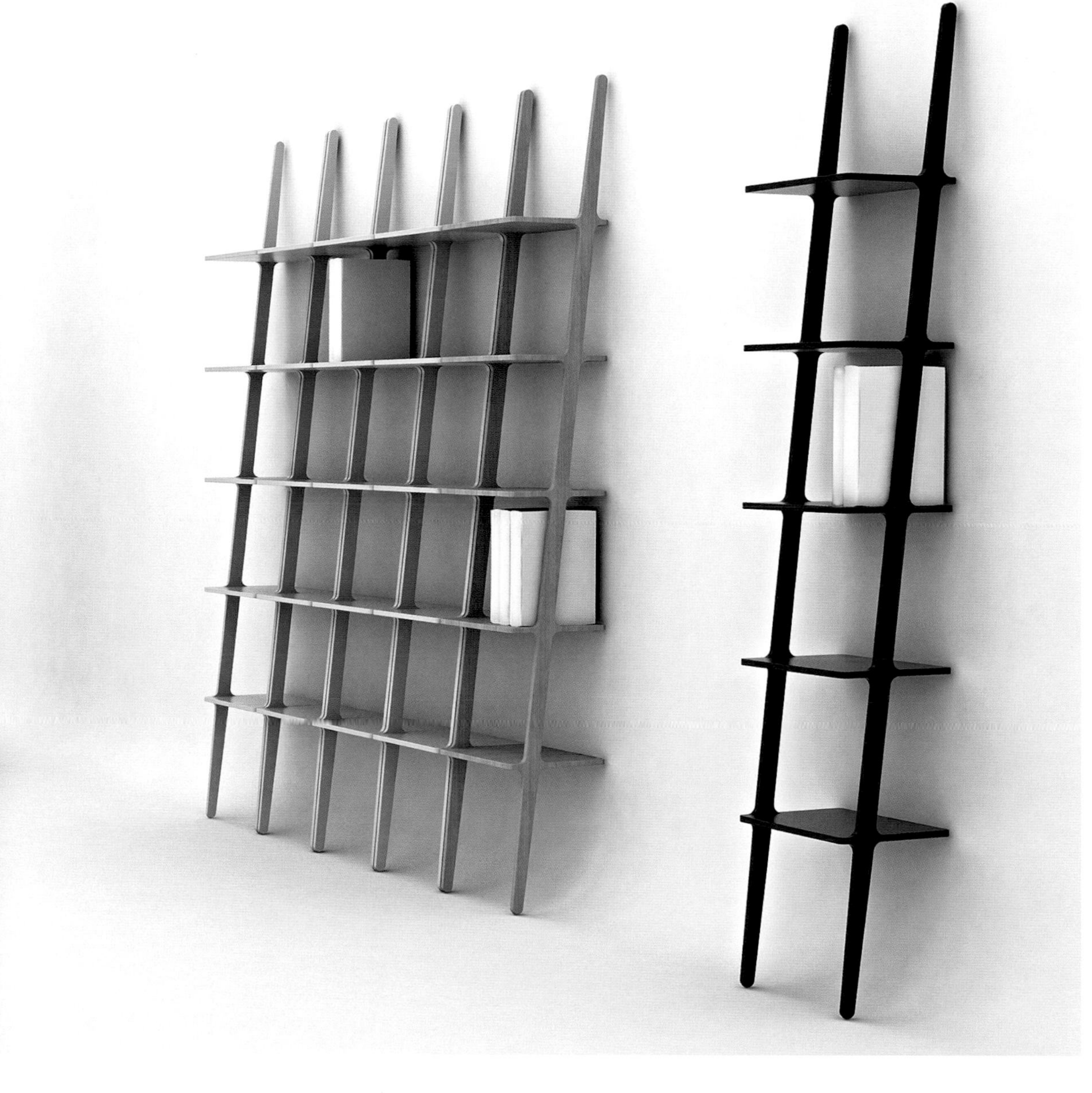

Parallel World collection

Material MDF
Dimensions Various

||||||||||||||||||||||||||||||||||||||||||||||||||||||||||||||||||||||||||||||||||||||||||||||||

Belarus-born, Paris-based designer Dzmitry Samal explains
'The Parallel World collection has a certain philosophical meaning,
as it reminds us about the possible existence of parallel worlds.
The presented pieces are partly hidden in nowhere, or held by
another world … '
www.samaldesign.com

Human Furniture collection

Materials Corian, or plastic and MDF
Dimensions Various
||||||||||||||||||||||||||||||||||||||||||||||||||||||||||||||||||||||||||||||
Samal goes on to say, 'The Human
Furniture collection was created as a mix
between the pragmatism and efficiency
of the geometrical shapes and sculptural
beauty of human body.'
www.samaldesign.com

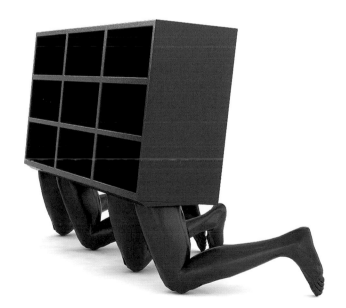

Sliding Shelves
Material Various woods
Dimensions Various

||||||||||||||||||||||||||||||||||||||||||||||||||||||||||||||||||||||||||||||||||||||||||||||||||||||||||

Sliding Shelves is a storage unit made from boxes of different
sizes and colours that can move along a wooden track attached
to the wall. The layout of Berlin-based architect and cabinetmaker
Lutz Hüning's design can easily be reconfigured.
www.lutzhuening.com

Parametric ∨
Material Lacquered MDF
Dimensions Various
||||||||||||||||||||||||||||||||||||||||||||||||||||||||||||||||||||||||||||
Each customer first selects their individual specifications (length, height and preferred colours) and Caterina Tiazzoldi's parametric system automatically changes some of the attributes (depth, thickness and colour saturation). The result is that every bookshelf is not only custom designed for its environment, but also entirely unique.
www.tiazzoldi.org

Sum ∧
Materials Cherry wood, brass fixings
Dimensions Various
||||||||||||||||||||||||||||||||||||||||||||||||||||||||||||||||||||||||||||
An asymmetrical shelving system that uses the same four angles in different combinations to create three unit shapes. These can then be built up together to form shelves of any size. The original designs were all handmade to order, and subsequently the production (by furniture manufacturer SCP) has aimed to replicate that feel.
www.petermarigold.com

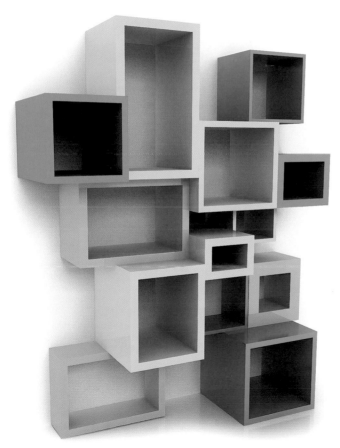

Playtime
Materials Carolina pine, thermo-coated aluminium
Dimensions 140 × 20 × 70 cm/ 55⅛ × 7⅞ × 27⅝ in.

A shelf inspired by Jacques Tati's 1967 film of the same name, in which the Monsieur Hulot character finds himself at odds with a futuristic society full of straight lines and modernist glass structures. Playtime's modules can be fixed at varying heights.
www.dustdeluxe.com

Bookspile

Material Plywood
Dimensions Various
|||||||||||||||||||||||||||||||||||||||||||||||||||||||||||||||||||||
This bookcase requires neither bolts, nails nor glue for assembly – just the integral 'fakebooks', which come in a variety of sizes. Lithuanian designer Andrius Pocius says 'The concept is based on the search for an ideal pile that can easily be created according to need or mood.'
www.andriuspocius.com

ABC

Material Lacquered wood
Dimensions 150 × 40 × 150 cm/
59 × 15¼ × 59 in.
||||||||||||||||||||||||||||||||||||||||||||||||||||||||||||||||||||||||||||||||||||||||||||||||||||
ABC is a freestanding rack with individual spaces for books of
varying sizes, but is particularly suitable for taller volumes. The
bookcase (available in a variety of colours) comes from Istanbul
design workshop Zift, and is designed by Lütfi Büyüktopbas.
www.ziftdesign.com

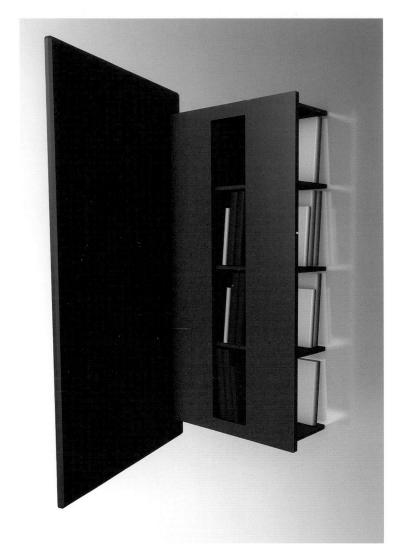

Les Dandys

Material Printed MDF
Dimensions 60 × 18 × 120 cm/
23⅜ × 7 × 47¼ in.
||||||||||||||||||||||||||||||||||||||||||||||||||||||||||||||||||||
Les Dandys by French design duo
Benoît and Rachel Convers is a range
of bookcases concealed by prints. Each
of the five designs in the collection has
been given a title inspired by famous
writers and novels of the 18th and
19th centuries. For example, 'Bel-Ami'
(opposite right above) is the title of
a novel by Guy de Maupassant, and
'Chatterton' (opposite right below) was
a well-known poet and literary forger.
www.ibride.fr

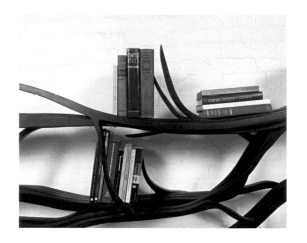

Metamorphosis

Material Baltic birch wood
Dimensions 320 × 37 × 140 cm/
126 × 14⅜ × 55⅛ in.

||||||||||||||||||||||||||||||||||||||||||||||||||||||||||||||||||||||||||||||||||||||||||||||||||||

The shelves of Sebastian Errazuriz's one-off, handcarved bookcase
perfectly evoke ivy's creeping habit. The particularly personal
design was inspired by the branches that grew on Sebastian's
childhood home in Santiago, Chile – branches that he and his
brothers used as shelves for their toys.

www.meetsebastian.com

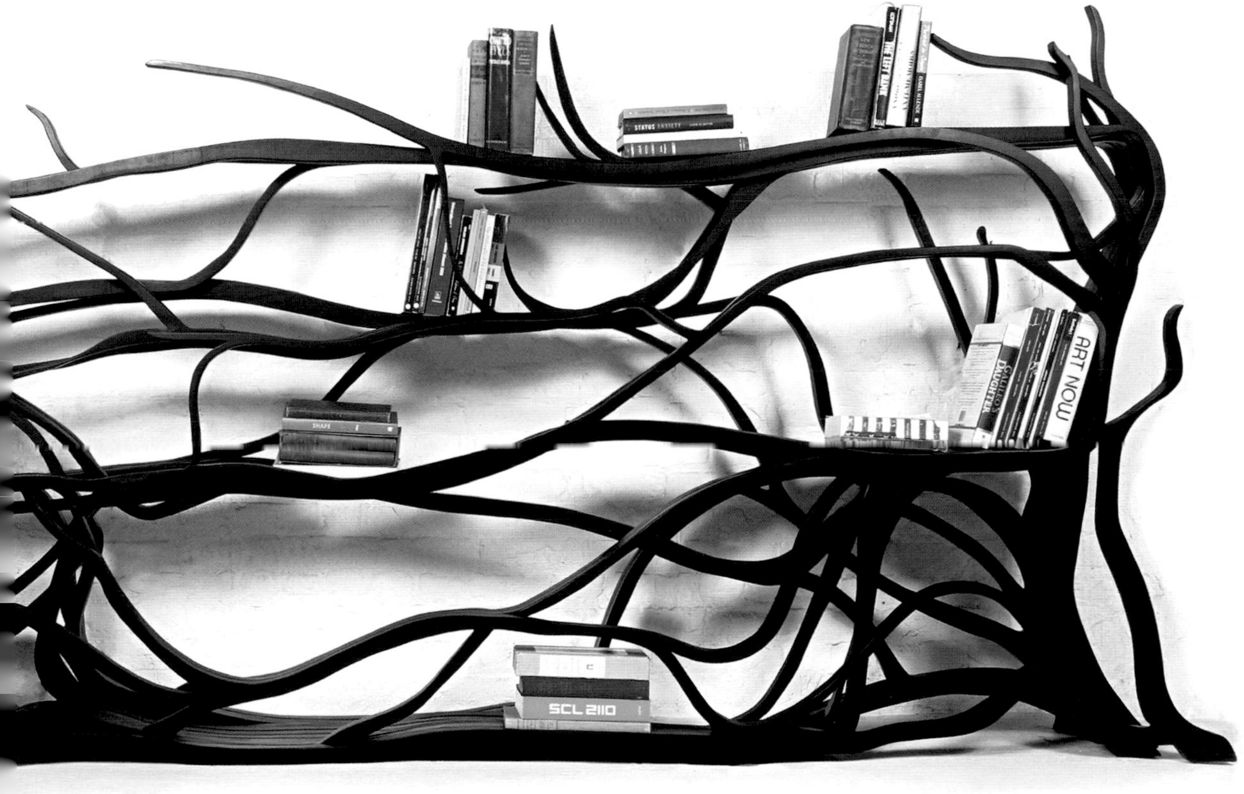
STATUS ANXIETY
THE LEFT BANK
GALILEO'S DAUGHTER
ART NOW
SHAPE
SCL 2110

Chaos Theory

Material Ash

Dimensions 130 × 45 × 170 cm/
51⅛ × 17¾ × 66¾ in.

|||||||||||||||||||||||||||||||||||||||||||||||||||||||||||||

Despite this bookcase's genuinely
worrying appearance, designer Manuel
Welsky says 'The crooked arrangement
ensures that the furniture stiffens on
its own, and is therefore able to resist
the burdens of even huge amounts
of books.' No tools are required to
assemble Chaos Theory.

www.welsky.net

FKY >>

Materials Oak and lacquered beech

Dimensions 200 × 35 × 200 cm/
78¾ × 13¾ × 78¾ in.

|||||||||||||||||||||||||||||||||||||||||||||||||||||||||||||

Sticks of varying widths and colours
are crossed in nine layers, with horizontal
ones parallel and vertical ones angled.
The interconnections serve to stabilize
the structure.

www.numen.eu

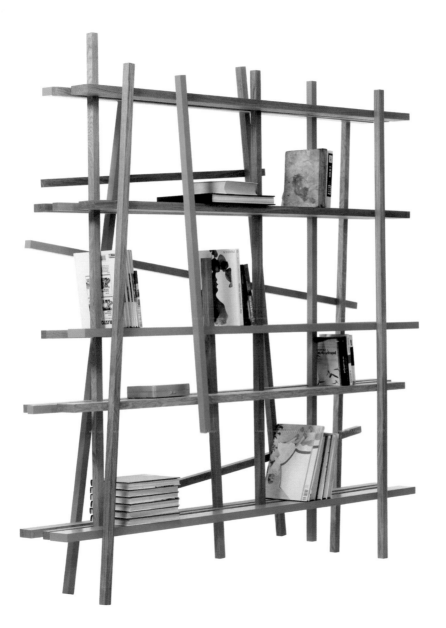

Bookmark

Material Lacquered MDF

Dimensions 60 × 30 × 50 cm/
23⅝ × 11¾ × 19¾ in.

||||||||||||||||||||||||||||||||||||||||||||||||||||||||||||||||||||||||||||||||||||||||||||||||||

Barbara Gollackner and Michael Walder's interlocking bookshelf is made up of identical constituent units that store books at a gentle angle. Lightweight, easy to stack and sturdy enough to lean against, when they appear together in numbers an eye-catching pattern is produced.

www.undpartner.at

Bookcase

Material Beech

Dimensions 200 × 44 × 50 cm/
78¾ × 17⅜ × 19¾ in.

||||||||||||||||||||||||||||||||||||||||||||||||||||||||||||||||||||||||||||||||||||||||||||||||||

Aïssa Logerot's limited-edition horizontal bookcase aims to
suggest a tree trunk sliced into planks. Placed in the middle of a
living room to create an island for readers, or used as a table or
bench, the design harks back to the earliest days of storing books.

www.aissalogerot.com

Vintage

Material MDF

Dimensions 100 × 31 × 190 cm/
39⅜ × 12¼ × 74⅞ in.

||||||||||||||||||||||||||||||||||||||||||||||||||||||||||||||||||||||||||||||||||||||||

Fusing stylish baroque-era design with contemporary simplicity,
the silhouette-effect Vintage from Munkii in Singapore plays with
the concept of space and negative space.

www.munkii.com.sg

Cell

Materials Steel, wire
Dimensions 50 × 21cm/
19¾ × 8¼ in.
||||||||||||||||||||||||||||||||||||||||||||||||||||||||||||||
The paper-thin shelves of Peter Cohen's
inconspicuous yet elegant shelf design
are remarkably strong and will not
bow. Metal strings interspersed with load-
bearing spheres hold the wall-mounted
units together. The height of the shelf
can be varied to suit its location.

www.string.se

Pogo Library

Materials Wood (maple, cherry, white oak or walnut), steel, rubber tips
Dimensions Various

||||||||||||||||||||||||||||||||||||||||||||||||||||||||||||||||||||||

Compression-fit poles mean no drilling is needed to install the Pogo Library bookcase: all Julie Scheu's design needs is a ceiling and a floor, meaning the shelves can also stand in the middle of rooms with ease.

www.juliescheu.com

Staircase >

Materials Bamboo, stainless steel
Dimensions 74 × 55 × 260 cm/ 29⅛ × 21⅝ × 102 in.

||||||||||||||||||||||||||||||||||||||||||||||||||||||||||||||||||||||

Danny Kuo believes the most efficient way to build is vertically: 'When it comes to living, the focus for the future is on height.' His pull-out stairs/ bookshelf design provides a solution to the problem of reaching books stowed out of arm's reach – simply step up on the bottom shelves.

www.dannykuo.com

A Medley of Bookcases

Ladder No. 1
Material Oak
Dimensions Various
||||||||||||||||||||||||||||||||||||||||||||||||||||||||||||
A ladder with rungs enlarged to
produce shelves has created what
designers Casimir describe as a 'stairway
upgrade'. On the largest models, a short
climb up the bottom shelves is necessary
to reach the books at the top.
www.casimirmeubelen.be

Sendai

Materials Laminated stainless steel, walnut, alder

Dimensions 120 × 42 × 190 cm/ 47¼ × 16⅝ × 74¾ in.

||||||||||||||||||||||||||||||||||||||||||||||||||||||||||||||||||||

A combination of bookcase and sculpture, the shelves represent water surfaces connected by reed stems. The shelves also form interesting reflected images when viewed from the side. The Sendai Mediatheque in Japan (another project designed by Toyo Ito) also uses this 'urban aquarium' effect.

www.toyo-ito.co.jp
www.horm.it

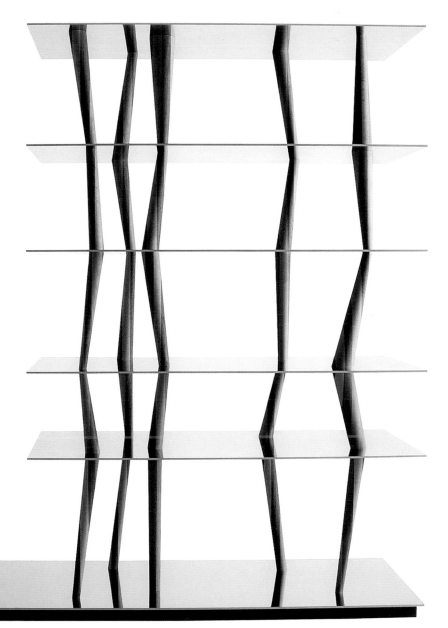

Shelf of Shelves
Materials Plywood, various veneers
Dimensions Various
||||||||||||||||||||||||||||||||||||||||||||||||||||||||||||||||||||||||
These four independent bookcases are in perfect proportion, but of diminishing size. The Shelf of Shelves, designed by Hans Tan, can be used as separate parts, or together in a variety of configurations.
www.hanstan.net

Pirouette

Materials Plywood, metal
Dimensions 140 × 30 × 180 cm/
55⅛ × 11⅞ × 70⅞ in.
||||||||||||||||||||||||||||||||||||||||||||||||||||||||||||||||||||||||
Jane Lioe's bookcase is inspired
by origami techniques, whereby a 3D
shape is formed from flat material.
Metal cylinder rings and pins enable the
shelf-columns to pivot out from one side.
www.coroflot.com/j_lioe

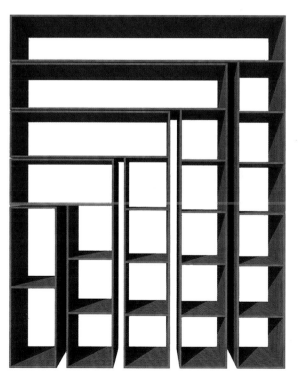

Mikado
Material Oak
Dimensions Various

||||||||||||||||||||||||||||||||||||||||||||||||||||||||||||||||||||||||||||||||||||||||||||||||||||||||||||

Jean-François Bellemère designed Mikado as both a bookshelf and a piece of art. The title of the design is a name commonly given to the game of pick-up sticks, and looking at the shape it's easy to see the association. Against such minimalist shelving, books appear to float off the wall.

www.editioncompagnie.fr

Laderszat

Materials Various woods
Dimensions Various

||||||||||||||||||||||||||||||||||||||||||||||||||||||||||||||||||||||||||||||||||||||||||||||||||||||

Everything in this design is held together by only two screws.
Chris Ruhe collects old, unsafe wooden ladders from Belgian
construction sites to make his Laderszat. He also uses old doors
and crates to create cabinets.

www.chrisruhe.nl

Varvis
Materials MDF, metal
Dimensions Various
||||||||||||||||||||||||||||||||||||||||||||||||||||||||||||||||||||||||||||||||||||||||||||||||||

'Life is a chaos,' say Swedish designers Mats Gylldorff and
Stina Svalin, 'So is our bookshelf. We didn't think outside
of the box. We just thought many boxes. Think of Varvis as
a rebel among bookshelves. Conformity is for cowards. Varvis
dares to be different and will recreate itself over time. Challenge
your creativity!'

www.gylldorffsvalin.com

Contrapunto
Materials Inlay (walnut, sycamore or cedar), metal fittings
Dimensions 290 × 45 × 225 cm/
114 × 17¾ × 88⅜ in.
||||||||||||||||||||||||||||||||||||||||||||||||||||||||||||||||||||||||||||||||||
This elegant bookshelf was designed by Barcelona-born
Jaime Tresserra to use only a minimal amount of materials.
Contrapunto is the Spanish for 'counterpoint', and there
is an agreeable mixture of independence and harmony
between the design elements.
www.tresserra.com

Twig
Material Powder-coated steel
Dimensions 51 × 20 × 127 cm/
20 × 8 × 50 in.
||||||||||||||||||||||||||||||||||||||||||||||||||||||||||||||||||||||||||||||||||||||
Faktura Design's elegant bookcase mimics the natural outlines of
branches. Designed by New Yorker Miron Lior, Twig is a bookshelf
without boards, meaning that both the covers and spines of your
favourite volumes can be seen. Other shelves by Miron Lior
are shown on pages 122 and 125.
www.fakturadesign.com

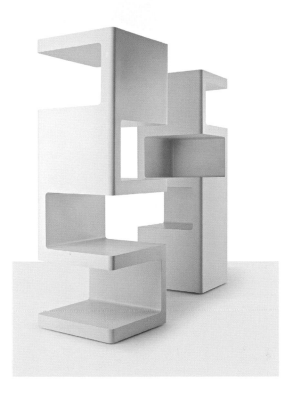

Face
Material Fibreglass
Dimensions 60 × 60 × 180 cm/
23⅜ × 23⅜ × 70⅞ in.
||||||||||||||||||||||||||||||||||||||||||||||||||||||||||||||||||||||||||||||||||||
Beautiful even when empty, Aziz Sarıyer's units allow books to be shelved facing in different directions. Castors make it simple to reposition the shelves within a room.
www.derindesign.com

Etagère KC
Materials Wood, metal or layered cardboard
Dimensions 110 × 35 × 190 cm/
43¼ × 13¾ × 74⅞ in.
||||||||||||||||||||||||||||||||||||||||||||||||||||||||||||||||||||||||||||||||||||
Although the lower shelves become increasingly less useful for storing books, the collapsed feel of the Etagère KC adds a unique visual touch to any library.
www.parsydebonsdesign.com

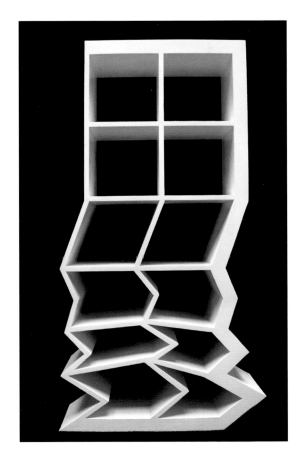

Pallet

Material Lacquered plywood
Dimensions Various

||||||||||||||||||||||||||||||||||||||||||||||||||||||||||||||||||||||||||||||||||||||||||||||||||||||||||||||||||||||||||||||||||||

Baita Design Studio of Rio de Janeiro were inspired both by stacks of pallets and the question of how to achieve a modern look using a minimum of raw materials. Although entirely stable, the result is a rather unsettling shelf to look at. Books can be stored both horizontally and vertically.

www.baitadesign.com

Weave

Material Rubber-painted stainless steel
Dimensions 38 × 38 × 160 cm/
14¾ × 14¾ × 63 in.

Flat steel bars run at right angles to create the Weave bookcase, by Japanese designer Chicako Ibaraki. The Mondrian-inspired appearance of the structure changes according to one's viewpoint, and rubber paint prevents the books – up to 200 – slipping off.
www.chicakoibaraki.com

Pimp My Billy range
Materials MDF, oak
Dimensions Various
www.ding3000.com

Stütze
||||||||||||||||||||||||||||||||||||||||||||||||||||||
A series of 'hacked' shelf designs created
to customize the hugely popular Billy
bookshelf from Ikea. Stütze is a small
plate that forces one leg of the bookcase
up to make bookends redundant.

Billy Heidenreich ∧
||||||||||||||||||||||||||||||||||||||||||||||||||||||||||||||||||||||||||||||
Billy Heidenreich adds a lectern to the middle shelf, handy for displaying more than just the spine of a beautiful book.

< Billy Wilder
||||||||||||||||||||||||||||||||||||||||||||||||||||||||||||||||||||||||||||||
Billy Wilder resembles a green branch, growing across the bookcase to hold titles at a number of unexpected angles. These three shelf designs are from Carsten Schelling, Sven Rudolph and Ralf Webermann, who together comprise the collective Ding 3000.

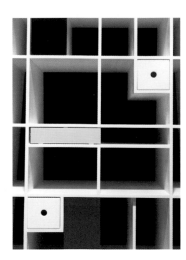

Moving Mondrian

Material Corian
Dimensions 100 × 48 × 190 cm/
39⅜ × 18⅞ × 74⅞ in.
||||||||||||||||||||||||||||||||||||||||||||||||||||||||||||
Architect Vladimír Ambroz's variation
on Piet Mondrian's grid-like paintings
has a series of colourful shelves, doors
and drawers for books, as well as wheels
for added manoeuvrability. Available
as part of a limited-edition series with
a certificate of authenticity.
www.amosdesign.eu

< P-Bookshelf

Material Tinted birch
Dimensions 65 × 30 × 190 cm/
23⅝ × 11¾ × 74¾ in.
||||||||||||||||||||||||||||||||||||||||||||||||||||||||||||
A bookshelf with a functioning clock
built in. The pendulum, however,
remains caught mid-swing. Designed
by Moscow-based Yar Rassadin.
www.rassadin.com

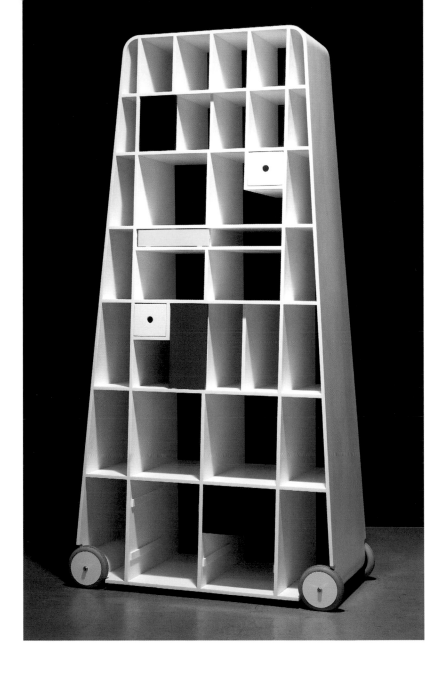

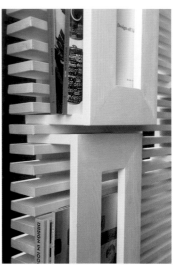

Pallet
Material Wood
Dimensions Various
||||||||||||||||||||||||||||||||||||||||||||||||||||||||||||||||||||||||
Flavia Dalla Pellegrina's rectangular
bookshelves attach to a large rack, and
can be moved around at will. The rack
itself is designed to be either wall
mounted, or used to divide a room.
Open fronts for some shelves mean
that books' covers can be as visible
as their spines.
www.flaviadallapellegrina.com

Lcdgc

Material MDF

Dimensions 110 × 39 × 210 cm/
43⅜ × 15⅜ × 82¾ in.

||||||||||||||||||||||||||||||||||||||||||||||||||||||||||||||||||||||||||||||||||||||||||||||||||

A slightly dizzying two- or four-column bookcase designed
by Kazuhiro Yamanaka. The structure, with its jutting, angled
shelves, was inspired by a steep rocky cliff rising out of the sea.
Two or more Ledge bookcases can be grouped to give an especially
vertiginous effect.

www.kazuhiroyamanaka.com

Storyteller ᵛ
Material Wood
Dimensions Various
||||||||||||||||||||||||||||||||||||||||||||||||||||||||||
Storyteller is made from old tables
that have been salvaged, sawn in half
and re-painted. Designer Isabel Quiroga
says, 'As the books are telling stories,
so would the tables if they could.'
www.isabelquiroga.com

Collect Shelf ᴧ
Materials Lacquer-stained pine
Dimensions 140 × 80 × 140 cm/
55¼ × 31½ × 55⅛ in.
||||||||||||||||||||||||||||||||||||||||||||||||||||||||||||||||
'We all have special objects that refresh
memories – things that have a meaning
and create the pleasure of recognition.
It could be anything from a football
to a stone found on a walk on a beach,'
explains Copenhagen-based designer
Ole Jensen, whose Collect shelf is
made for memorable books.
www.olejensendesign.com

Torres de Satélite

Materials Plywood with walnut veneer
Dimensions Various
||||||||||||||||||||||||||||||||||||||||||||||||||||||||
These five bookshelves by the NEL
collective (Ricardo Casas, Alejandro
Castro, Héctor Esrawe, Emiliano Godoy
and Cecilia León de la Barra) are homage
to the Torres de Satélite (Satellite Towers)
in Ciudad Satélite, in the northern part
of Naucalpan de Juárez, Mexico City.
The shelves have been painted in
colours similar to the original
monuments. Another design by
NEL appears on page 225.
www.nel.com.mx

Twin Shelves

Material Lacquered MDF
Dimensions 93 × 30 × 180 cm/
36⅝ × 11¾ × 70⅞ in.
‖‖

A bookcase featuring irregular oval-
shaped spaces for books and other objects
by gt2P, a parametric design and digital
fabrication studio based in Santiago,
Chile. The shelves are part of a series
of furniture designed using an algorithm
based on a Voronoi tessellation.
www.gt2p.com

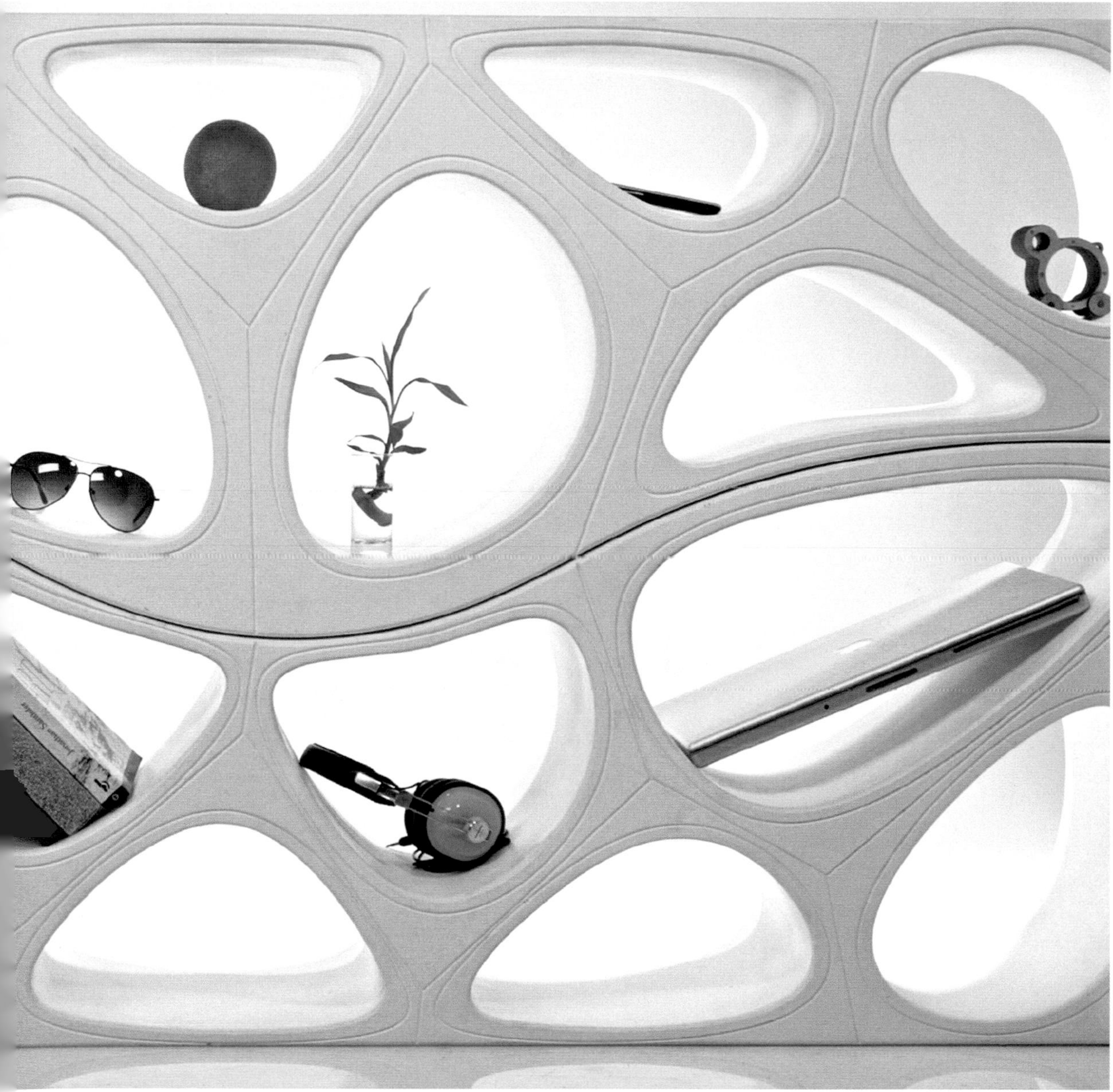

Comb

Material Birch plywood
Dimensions 220 × 40 × 220 cm/
86⅝ × 15¾ × 86⅝ in.
||||||||||||||||||||||||||||||||||||||||||||||||||||||||||||||||||
This bookcase seems to bulge from the
wall, providing a science-fiction backdrop
for the volumes it holds. Designer Jaanus
Orgusaar points out that the film-coated
waterproof plywood is easy to clean, and
that the whole can be flat packed.
www.jaanusorgusaar.com

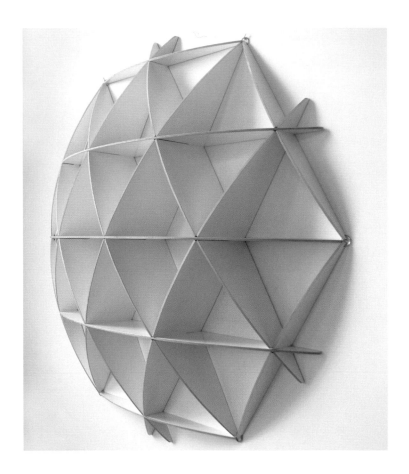

Puckman
Material Varnished wood
Dimensions 165 × 50 × 180 cm/
64¼ × 19¾ × 70¾ in.
|||||||||||||||||||||||||||||||||||||||||||||||||||||||||||||||||||||||
Alessandra Papazzo's striking bookcase is
a tribute to the cult 1980s video game of
nearly the same name. Available in yellow,
white or black.
www.ginepro.org

Kaos
Material MDF
Dimensions 180 × 40 × 120 cm/
70⅞ × 15¾ × 47¼ in.
||||||||||||||||||||||||||||||||||||||||||||||||||||||||||||||||||
Rather than classify books alphabetically
or by genre, the maze-like Kaos
encourages the book owner to store
them in small groups; a feature that
designer Thomas Neuber says means
various organizational systems can
function alongside each other. The result
is a chaotic 3D picture composed
of books.
www.destilat.at

Pile Up

Material Steel
Dimensions 170 × 50 × 120 cm/
66⅞ × 19¾ × 47¼ in.
||||||||||||||||||||||||||||||||||||||||||||||||||||||||||||||||||||||||||||||||||||||||||||||||||||||||
A minimalist bookcase for those who like to see an element of
accident in their book display. The designers, MicroWorks, claim
that 'books randomly piled up have unique beauty'. The shaped
steel acts as a built-in bookend on one side, keeping things in hand.
www.microworks.jp

< Stacked

Material Birch
Dimensions Various
||||||||||||||||||||||||||||||||||||||||||||||||||||||||
Bookcase No. 11 and Cabinet No. 7 are
part of a series of abstract, Dalí-esque
furniture designs by Vincent Leman
from Valparaiso, Indiana. The pieces
are finished in environmentally friendly
paints and then distressed by hand.
www.dustfurniture.com

Factor

Material Ebonized teak
Dimensions 80 × 60 × 220 cm/
31½ × 23⅝ × 86⅝ in.
|||||||||||||||||||||||||||||||||||||||||||||||||||||||||||||||
An attractive, ergonomic bookcase
designed to encompass a natural arc,
based on the eye-line and reach of readers
searching for books. Slight lips prevent
the books falling down. Designer
Jonathan Olivares points out that when
positioned in facing rows the cases form
a tunnel, surrounding browsers inside.
www.jonathanolivares.com

Fluid
Materials Steel rods, sheet metal, transparent plastic joints
Dimensions 27 × 42 × 35 cm/
10⅝ × 16⅝ × 13¾ in.
||||||||||||||||||||||||||||||||||||||||||||||||||||||||||||||||||||||||||||||||||||||||||||||||||
A modular bookcase with a caged and sturdy aspect, designed
by Arik Levy for Desalto. The company says that the Fluid
project 'explores infinite spatial possibilities through a single
element, mimicking DNA by allowing the generation
of endless combinations.'
www.desalto.it

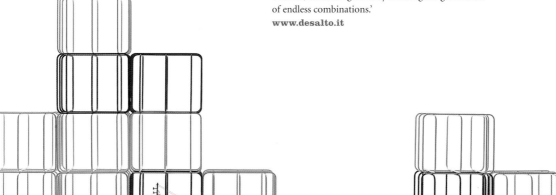

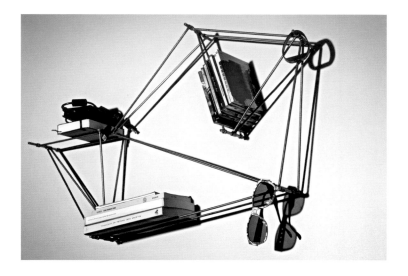

Tensor Voting
Material Iron rods
Dimensions Various
||||||||||||||||||||||||||||||||||||||||||||||||||||||||||||||||
A skeletal bookcase built using iron rods
of different length that are slotted into
fasteners and then attached to the wall.
Swiss designer Guilio Parini's creation
can easily be extended and adjusted.
www.giulioparini.blogspot.com

Director >
Materials Powder-coated steel, glass
Dimensions 45 × 45 × 210 cm/
17¾ × 17¾ × 82¾ in.
||||||||||||||||||||||||||||||||||||||||||||||||||||||||||||||||
Niko Economidis is based in Greenpoint,
Brooklyn. He describes his Director
design as a 'physical line drawing'
of an antique bookcase. Although
perfectly serviceable as individual units,
the two halves of the case have greater
visual strength when paired up.
The Read-Unread bookshelf on
page 201 is by the same designer.
www.nikoeconomidis.com

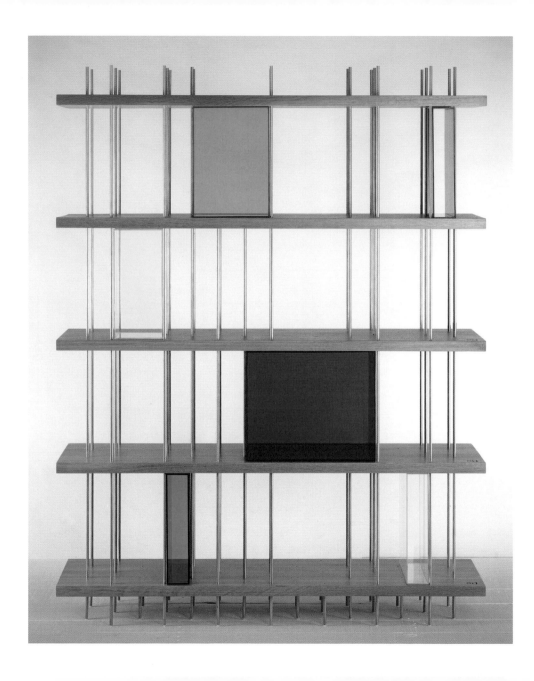

< Çok Çok

Materials Plexiglas, wood, brass, steel
Dimensions 220 × 33 × 110 cm/
86⅝ × 13 × 43⅜ in.
||||||||||||||||||||||||||||||||||||||||||||||||||||||||||||||||||||||||||||||||||
Istanbul-based Serhan Gurkan's Çok Çok (Turkish for 'More
More') is based on the designer's principle that one should
'play with less to create more'. Numerous thin steel rods hold
the shelves together, giving a light and airy feel.
www.serhangurkan.com

Circus

Materials Oak, powder-coated steel
Dimensions 240 × 36 × 54 cm/
94½ × 14¼ × 21¼ in.
||||||||||||||||||||||||||||||||||||||||||||||||||||||||||||||||||||||||||||||||||
Designed by Stephen Burks, Circus is inspired by the jollity
of the big top. Each shelf is supported by up to eight coloured-
wire cages that plug into the surface of the shelf below – so no
tools are needed for construction. As well as supporting the
bookshelves, the cages make ideal sites for displaying favourite
objects. The dimensions above are per shelf.
www.mattermatters.com

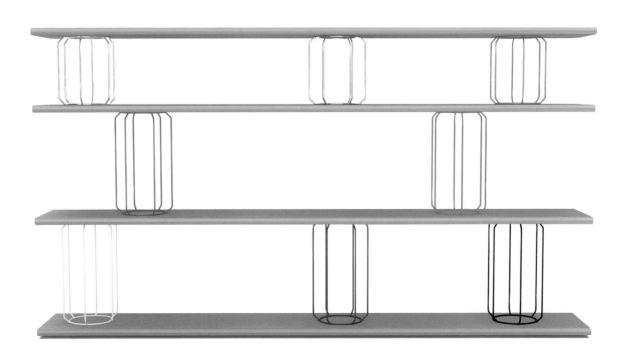

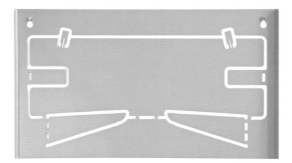

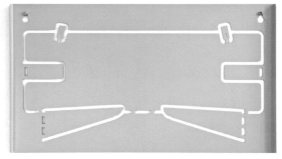

Piegato One
Material Powder-coated steel
Dimensions 66 × 2 × 100 cm/
26 × ¾ × 39⅜ in.

||||||||||||||||||||||||||||||||||||||||||||||||||||||||||||||||||||||||||||||||||||||||||||||||||||||||||||

Constructing the Piegato One requires only a single pre-cut sheet
of steel, which can be easily bent by hand to form bookshelves
when required. The shelf, designed by Matthias Ries, comes
in a range of six colours, and doubles as a board for magnets.
Another Matthias Ries bookshelf design, the Plus One,
can be seen on page 258.
www.matthiasries.com
www.mrdoproducts.com

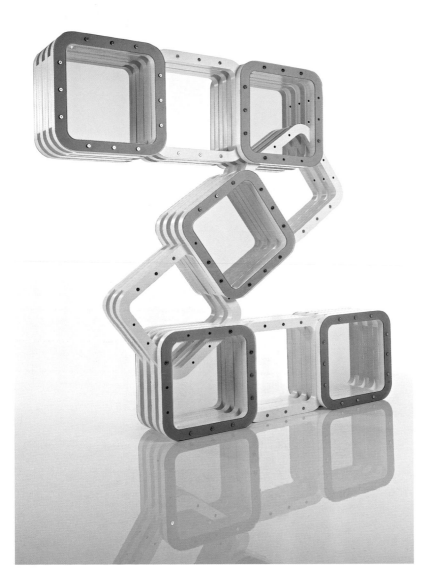

More

Materials Recycled wood
or cardboard
Dimensions 45 × 5 × 45 cm/
17¾ × 2 × 17¾ in.
||||||||||||||||||||||||||||||||||||||||||||||||||||||||||||||||
The More units fasten together using
special pins and threaded ropes, allowing
endless arrangements of shelves, seats
and platforms. They can even be hung
from the ceiling. According to its designer
Giorgio Caporaso, 'More is the response
to everyday life that demands an ongoing
flexibility of spaces and adaptability
of furniture to meet the ongoing changes
in lifestyle.' The measurements above
are given per unit.
www.caporasodesign.it

More

(See previous page for details.)
|||||||||||||||||||||||||||||||||||||||||||||||||||||||||||
More is easy to assemble and comes
in recyclable wood or cardboard.
The modules can be rearranged
to form diagonal, vertical and
horizontal bookshelves.

Quetza

Materials Birch plywood, biodegradable finish
Dimensions 54 × 21 × 100 cm/
21¼ × 8¼ × 39⅜ in.

|||||||||||||||||||||||||||||||||||||||||||||||||||||||||||||||||||||||||||||||||||||||||||

Quetza looks like a snake sliding down a staircase for good reason – it is designed to resemble historic depictions of the Mesoamerican deity Quetzalcoatl. The ancient god appeared in the shape of a feathered serpent, and was particularly associated with linking the sky and earth.

www.nel.com.mx
www.pirwi.com

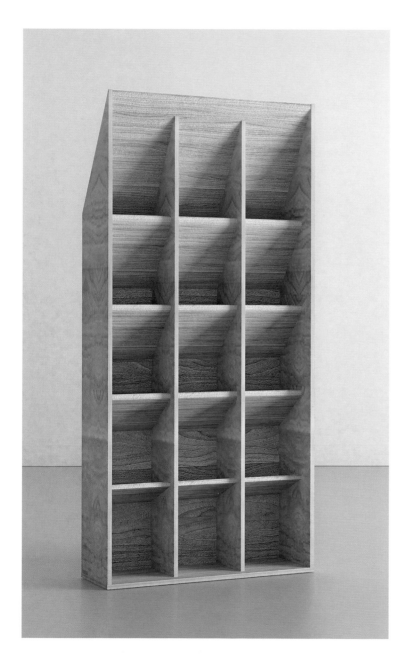

Perspective Shelf
Material Oak
Dimensions Various
||||||||||||||||||||||||||||||||||||||||||||||||||||||||||||||||||
Fuquan Junze designed this bookcase
according to the principles of perspective
drawing. The visual effect works
irrespective of whether the case
is installed vertically or horizontally.
www.oilmonkey.com

6 Degree >
Materials Wood
Dimensions Various
|||||||||||||||||||||||||||||||||||||||||||||||||||||||||||||||||||||||||
A modular, mathematical shelving system:
two blocks placed horizontally on each
other equal the height of one module
in an upright position, while the
eponymous '6' is the number of degrees
that separate it from a right angle.
www.lovekompott.com

Dickens

Material Layered cardboard
Dimensions 55 × 35 × 150 cm/
21⅜ × 13¾ × 59 in.
||||||||||||||||||||||||||||||||||||||||||||||||||||||||||||||||
The lightweight retro-futuristic Dickens
by Reinhard Dienes is completely
recyclable and has a mixture of shelf sizes,
accommodating reading material from
magazines to mammoth tomes.
www.reinharddienes.com

Hex

Materials MDF, wallpaper
Dimensions Various
||||||||||||||||||||||||||||||||||||||||||||||||||||||||||||||||
A bookcase of six-sided units
(with interiors decorated in durable,
hand-printed wallpapers) that are custom
made to fit clients' colour schemes and
spaces. Tim Forrester's design can be
easily stacked in a honeycomb formation,
or instead used for stand-alone storage.
www.timothybenfurniture.co.uk

Pattern

Material Aluminium composite
Dimensions Various

||||||||||||||||||||||||||||||||||||||||||||||||||||||||||||||||

Designed by Alfredo Häberli, who
used irregular pentagons to create
this sculptural space for storing books
and exhibiting objects. A winner of
Wallpaper* magazine's 'Best Shelving
of the Year' accolade.
www.quodes.com

< Pyramid

Materials Anodized extruded
aluminium, MDF
Dimensions Various

||||||||||||||||||||||||||||||||||||||||||||||||||||||||||||||||

A modular, pyramidal bookcase designed
for office areas, but also perfectly suitable
for domestic spaces too. The Mini model
is less than 2 metres (6.5 ft) wide, while
the larger units can be up to 7.3 metres
(24 ft) wide, and 4.1 metres (13 ft 6 in.)
high. The units are available in silver,
white and black, and can be freestanding
or fixed to a wall.
www.fittingfitting.it

Upside Down

Materials Polyurethane cushions, stainless steel

Dimensions Various

||||||||||||||||||||||||||||||||||||||||||||||||||||||||||||||||||||

A suspended bookcase made using transparent, inflatable cushions and specialized lifting straps; when installed the shelves resemble the bar lines of a musical score. Upside Down was designed by Adrien de Melo for the Espace culturel Louis Vuitton in Paris, curated by Galerie BSL.

www.adriendemelo.com

Untamed Chaos

Material Wood
Dimensions 90 × 90 × 120 cm/
35½ × 35½ × 47¼ in.
||||||||||||||||||||||||||||||||||||||||||||||||||||||||||||||||||||||||
A freestanding bookcase made up of nine
identically sized boxes, stacked and angled
in a chaotic fusion by Hamburg designers
Daniel and Rosemarie Bormann.
Untamed Chaos was made available
in a limited edition of just fifteen.
www.bormann-design-art.de

Equilibrium
Material Wood
Dimensions 61 × 35 × 190 cm/
24 × 13¾ × 74⅞ in.

||||||||||||||||||||||||||||||||||||||||||||||||||||||||||||||||||||||||||||||||||||||||||||||||||||||||||||||||||

Colombia-born Alejandro Gomez Stubbs, the designer of Equilibrium, says 'The concept
was to design a piece that contrasted stylish modern design with playfulness and animation.'
www.malaganadesign.com

BarDeco

Materials Powder-coated steel, oak wood
Dimensions 24 × 28 × 210 cm/
9½ × 11 × 82¾ in.

Lina Meier's bookcase is inspired by the ubiquitous barcode.
The differing sizes of the slots means that books can be arranged
in both upright and flat positions, while the smaller niches are
useful for storing magazines. BarDeco is part of a collection
themed around the barcode, which includes a lampshade
and coat hooks.
www.linameier.com

Bookshelf/Sculpture >>

Material Powder-coated steel
Dimensions 20 × 20 × 150 cm/
7⅞ × 7⅞ × 59 in.

A bookshelf tower with individual recesses for books of varying
sizes. Through his designs, Rick Ivey hopes to 'challenge
preconceived ideas of what furniture is, and what it can be.'
Comes in black, white and rust colours.
www.rickivey.com

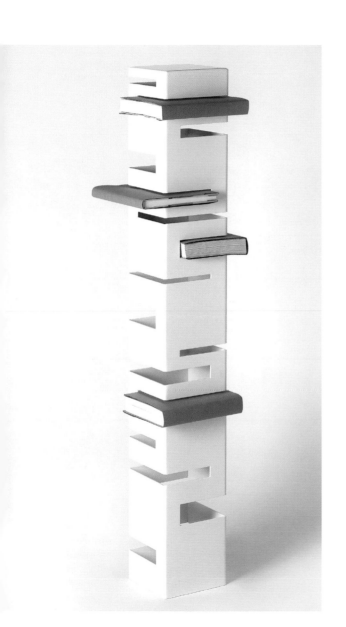

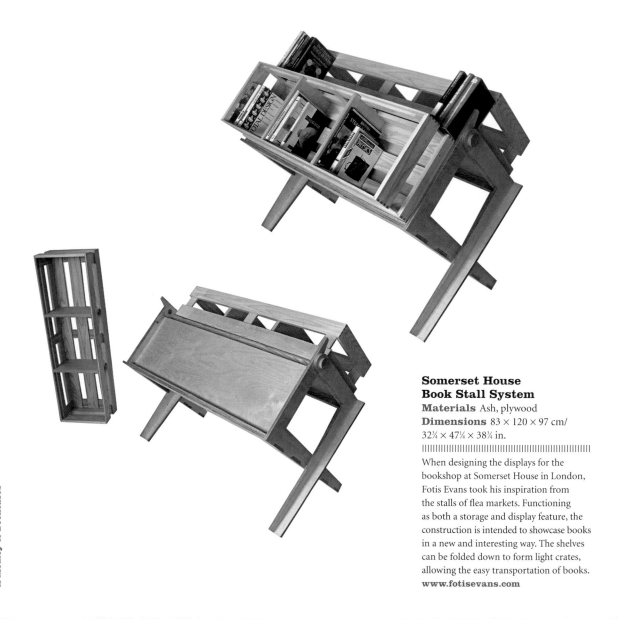

Somerset House
Book Stall System
Materials Ash, plywood
Dimensions 83 × 120 × 97 cm/
32¾ × 47¼ × 38¾ in.
||||||||||||||||||||||||||||||||||||||||||||||||||||||||||||||||||
When designing the displays for the
bookshop at Somerset House in London,
Fotis Evans took his inspiration from
the stalls of flea markets. Functioning
as both a storage and display feature, the
construction is intended to showcase books
in a new and interesting way. The shelves
can be folded down to form light crates,
allowing the easy transportation of books.
www.fotisevans.com

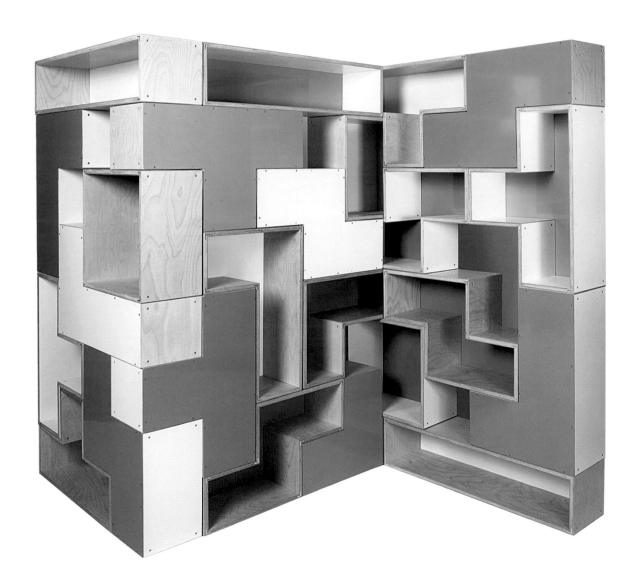

Tetrad

Materials Walnut, ash, coloured metal backings
Dimensions Various

||||||||||||||||||||||||||||||||||||||||||||||||||||||||||

Modular, reversible and interchangeable, these iconically shaped blocks offer a variety of bookshelf configurations.

The Tetrad designs feature front and back edges that are bevelled away from the interior surfaces, lending them an intriguing optical quality when viewed at an angle.

www.bravespacedesign.com

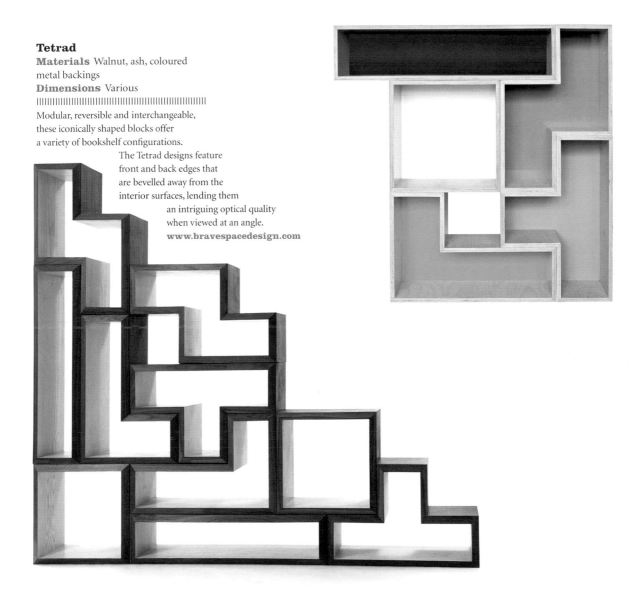

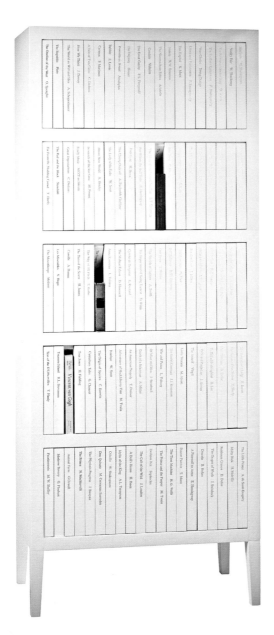

Ready Made

Materials MDF, leather, gold tooling
Dimensions 220 × 90 × 45 cm/
86⅝ × 35½ × 17¾ in.

||||||||||||||||||||||||||||||||||||||||||||||||||||||||

The Ready Made bookcase from
Amsterdam designers Next Architects
features a façade that consists of the
spines of 100 classic books, which you
can gently press in and replace with the
actual book once you have purchased it
(or simply insert your favourite volumes
and use the classic titles as bookends).
www.nextarchitects.com

Graffititek >

Materials Plywood, polyethylene
lighting
Dimensions 100 × 25 × 100 cm/
39⅜ × 9¾ × 39⅜ in.

||||||||||||||||||||||||||||||||||||||||||||||||||||||||

An integrated light illuminates this
many-angled bookshelf. Designer Charles
Kalpakian (from the Hello Karl studio in
Paris) was inspired by urban graffiti and
Kahlil Gibran's maxim from *The Prophet*:
'Charge all things you fashion with
a breath of your own spirit.'
www.hellokarl.com

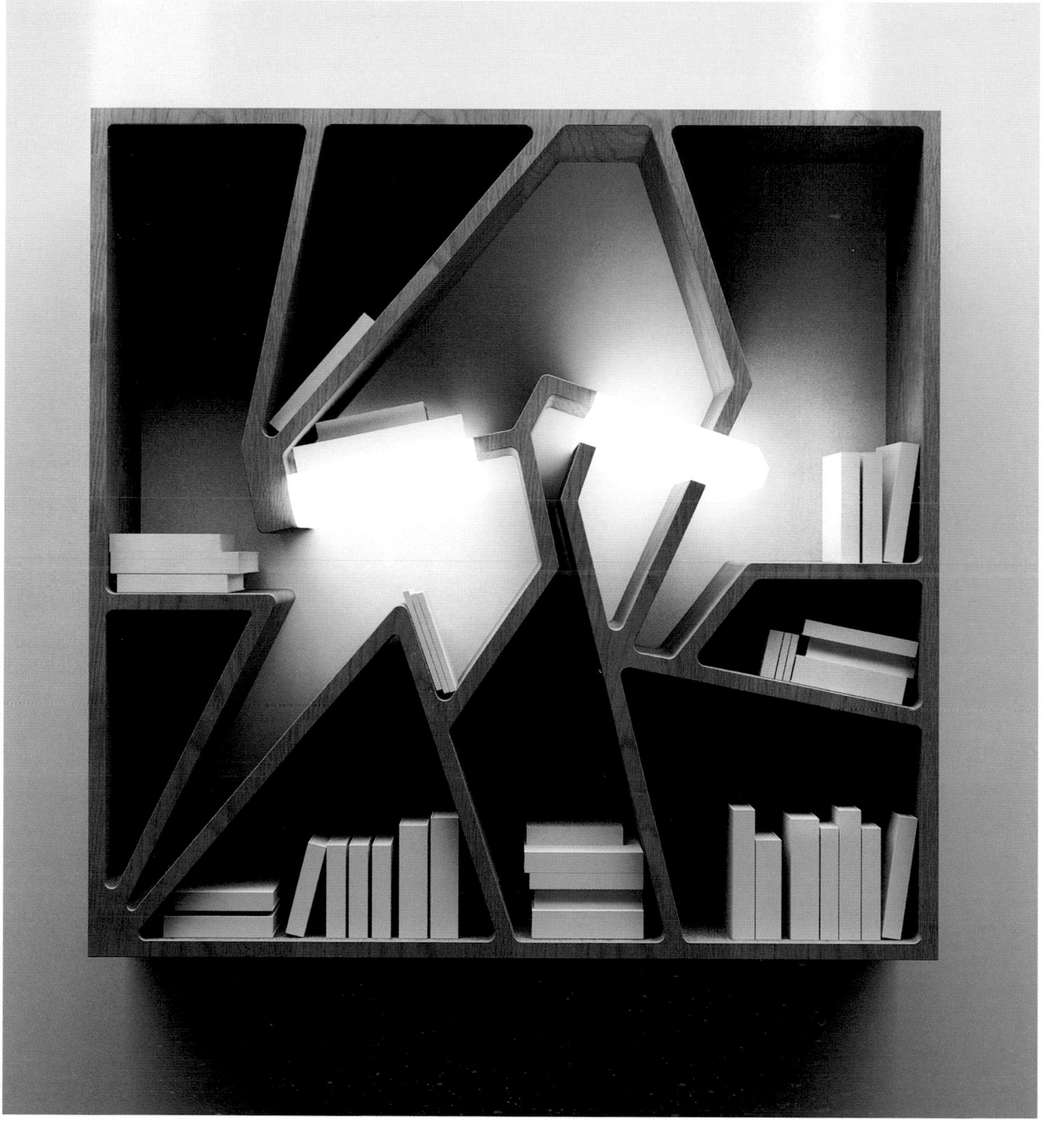

Quby
Material Rotomoulded polyethylene
Dimensions 33 × 44 × 44 cm/
13 × 17¼ × 17¼ in.
||||||||||||||||||||||||||||||||||||||||||||||||||||||||||||||
Colourful squareish book-storage blocks
that can be placed on the floor, stacked
or hung on walls. The inbuilt divider and
the slight angle of the shelves draws the
eye when a number are stacked together.
www.b-line.it

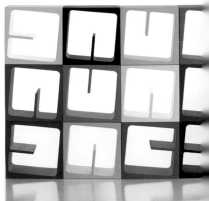

Zig Zag

Material Lacquered MDF

Dimensions 83 × 46 × 200 cm/
32¾ × 18¼ × 78¾ in.

||||||||||||||||||||||||||||||||||||||||||||||||||||||||||||||||||||||||||||||||||||

Aziz Sariyer's self-standing Zig Zag makes the most of difficult
corner spaces, and creates a rippled effect when three or more
are placed next to each other. Units can be joined together to
make a room divider, or, alternatively, four may be placed back
to back to produce a circular bookcase column.

www.b-line.it

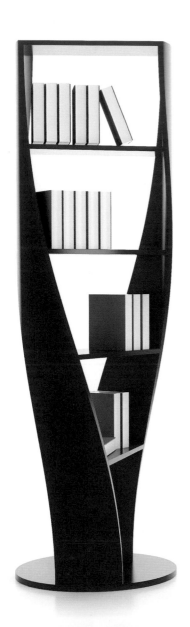

< MYDNA

Materials Plywood, cardboard
Dimensions Various

|||||||||||||||||||||||||||||||||||||||||||||||||||||||||||||||||||

MYDNA by Mexican designer Joel
Escalona is inspired by the double-helix
structure of DNA, an association
implying that the books you store in
it are an integral part of who you are.
www.joelescalona.com

Bookshape

Material Acrylic
Dimensions Various

|||||||||||||||||||||||||||||||||||||||||||||||||||||||||||||||||||

A series of laser-cut acrylic layers –
the inner ones white opal, the exterior
ones transparent and coloured – are
built up to form a bright bookcase
that silhouettes the shapes of volumes
on a shelf. Designer Davide Radaelli
comments, 'The original idea was that the
content had to give shape to its container.'
www.davideradaelli.com

Set 26

Material Wood
Dimensions Various

||||||||||||||||||||||||||||||||||||||||||||||||||||||||||

What do your bookshelves say about you?
All 26 letters of the alphabet (as well
as the plus sign and full stop) are rendered
as letter furniture, with doors that open
to reveal up to five shelves. Designer Erich
Keller and Set 26 invite you to buy your
favourite word.

www.set26.ch

Paperback

Material High-pressure laminate
Dimensions Various

||||||||||||||||||||||||||||||||||||||||||||||||||||||||||

A striking throwback to the early days
of the bookcase, when volumes were
stored horizontally, Paperback is a series
of wall plates with horizontal slots into
which shelves can be fitted at different
intervals. The shelves are a laminate
made from layers of kraft paper
impregnated with phenolic resin
and bonded by heat and pressure.
www.studioparade.nl

Rek

Material MDF

Dimensions 190 × 36 × 220 cm/
74⅞ × 14¼ × 86⅝ in.
||||||||||||||||||||||||||||||||||||||||||||||||||||||||||||||||
A bookcase that expands like an
accordion as your collection grows.
The interlocking zigzag elements slide
in and out, so that Rek is always 'full',
however few volumes you store. The
distinctive stepped pattern encourages
readers to shelve their books according
to size, creating an interesting visual
effect. The dimensions above describe
the maximum extent of the Rek, which
comes in light, medium and dark grey,
as well as white.
www.reinierdejong.com

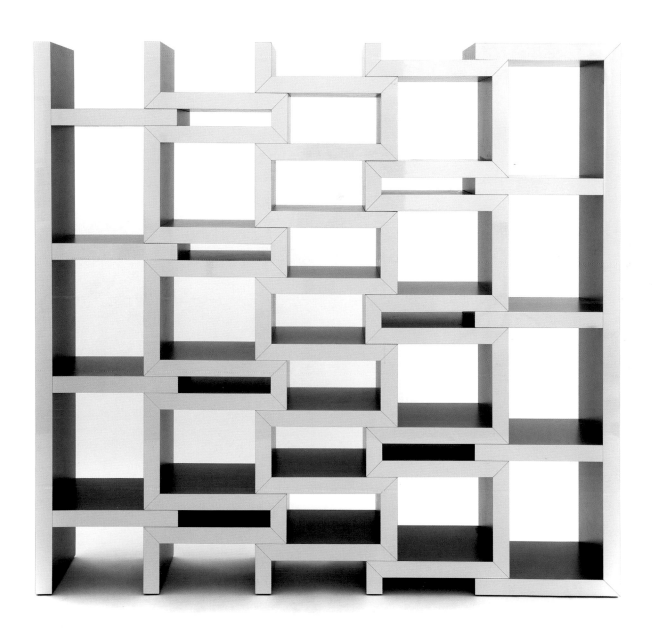

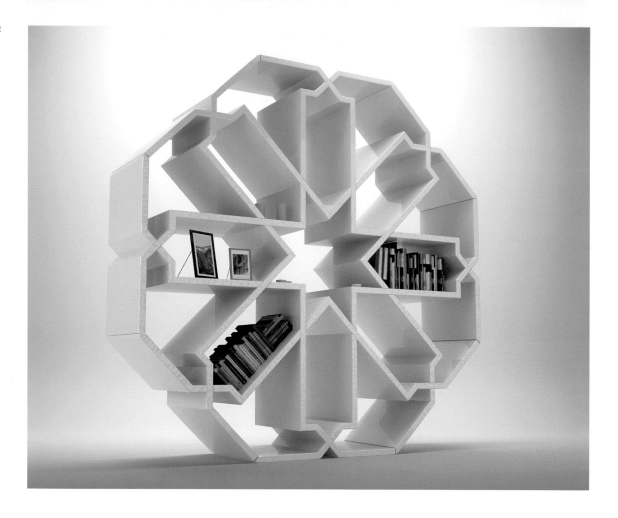

Zelli and MiniZelli
Material Simopor
Dimensions Various

|||||||||||||||||||||||||||||||||||||||||||||||||||||||||||||||||||||||||||||||||||||||||||||||||||||||||||||||||||||||||||||||||||||||||||||||||||||||||||||||||||||||||||||||||||||||||||||||||||

Zelli and MiniZelli are inspired by the zellige mosaics that designer Younes Duret
remembers seeing on living-room walls during his childhood in Morocco. The shelves
are constructed using eight identical sections that fit together clockwise, locked together
without nails or screws.

www.younesdesign.com

part 2/

A Cornucopia
of Designs

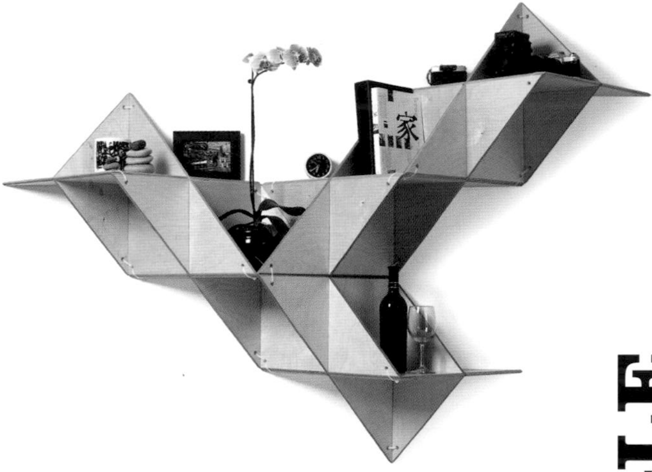

2 / SINGLE SHELVES

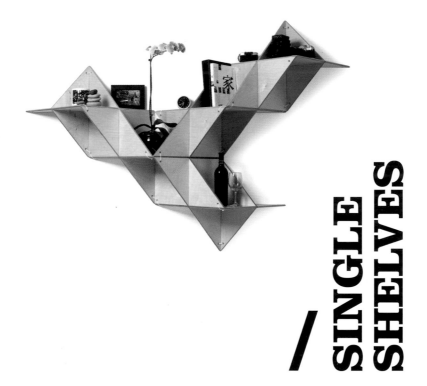

The Harvard Shelf – an anthology of 51 classic works of literature that would fit on a shelf 1.5 metres (5 ft) long – may be becoming a less common feature in the 21st-century home, but the single shelf itself remains the basic building block of book storage. Moreover, the shelf is arguably the aspect that allows designers the most scope to re-imagine the way we keep books. Unusual designs can be especially appealing, turning the humble bookshelf into both an important part of the interior decor and a talking point. Barok (page 127) and Comic (page 123) do this particularly well, the former literally framing the books and turning them into works of art, the latter underlining that books in the 21st century still have the power to talk to us.

The beauty of many of these shelves is that, while they work well individually, they are more eye-catching when arranged in groups (like books themselves). Even individuals who are not great readers, or who prefer e-books and have downsized their physical book collection, will still need shelves around the house for the occasional book, trinket or framed photograph. And after all, even if you have an e-book reader, you still need a shelf to keep it on …

City
Material Lacquered steel
Dimensions 80 × 14 × 24 cm/
31½ × 5½ × 9 in.
||||||||||||||||||||||||||||||||||||||||||||||||||||||||||||||||||||
This simple but attractive shelf is suited
to lighter possessions, such as paperbacks,
CDs and DVDs.
www.carl.hagerling.se

Storylines

Material Aluminium

Dimensions 90 × 20 × 28 cm/
35½ × 7⅞ × 11 in.

||||||||||||||||||||||||||||||||||||||||||||||||||||||||||||||||

Frederik Roijé says his bookshelf
is 'storytelling translated into a storage
function'. The shape is inspired by
the sine waves created by the sound
of the word 'bliss', and by the silhouette
of skyscrapers.

www.roije.com

Cumulus

Material Lacquered steel
Dimensions 80 × 14 × 24 cm/
31½ × 5½ × 9 in.
||||||||||||||||||||||||||||||||||||||||||||||||||||||||||||||||||||||||||||||||||||||||||||||
Carl Hagerling's Cumulus and City (page 118) designs can be
combined to create a metropolitan skyline topped with fluffy clouds.
www.dskmtg.com

Catalyst

Material Silicon
Dimensions Various

||||||||||||||||||||||||||||||||||||||||||||||||||||||||||||||

'My shelves aim to invite the user to interact with their form,' says Ji Young Seo. 'They utilize various "play signals" that encourage the user to touch, feel and react to the object.' Catalyst has a thin flap of silicon to hold your books in place.

www.jiyoungseo.tumblr.com

Z Shelf

Material Powder-coated steel
Dimensions 61 × 25 × 30 cm/
24 × 10 × 12 in.

‖‖‖

Designed by Miron Lior (who also
created the Twig bookcase on page 54),
the Z Shelf seems to hold books at
impossible angles. Two tiny hooks hold
the lower cover of the bottom book,
rendering the shelf inside invisible.
www.mironlior.com

Comic

Materials Lacquered MDF
Dimensions Various
||||||||||||||||||||||||||||||||||||||||||||||||||||||||||||||||
Comic, designed by Oscar Nuñez,
really brings books into the conversation.
The shelf works especially well when
appropriate works of art are hung
underneath.
www.fusca.mx

Conceal Shelf

Material Powder-coated steel
Dimensions 13 × 14 × 13 cm/
5¼ × 5½ × 5¼ in.

||||||||||||||||||||||||||||||||||||||||||||||||||||||||||||||

Another Miron Lior design that appears
to disregard gravity; books stacked on
the Conceal shelf seem to be floating in
mid-air. Like the Z Shelf, hooks hold the
cover of the bottom book to screen the
metal plate that bears the weight. If
additional books are piled on it, the
bracket that attaches the shelf to the
wall is also hidden.

www.mironlior.com

Stick

Material Lacquered steel
Dimensions Various

||||||||||||||||||||||||||||||||||||||||||||||||||||||||||

These simple yet stylish bookshelves
are designed by Clotilde de Grave
and Didier Chaudanson of Presse Citron.
Each bookshelf resembles a picture frame
and is open at the side, allowing light
to enter from the back.

www.presse-citron.com

Barok
Material Lacquered steel
Dimensions Various
||||||||||||||||||||||||||||||||||||||||||||||||||||||||||||||||||||||
Also from Presse Citron, these ornately
baroque black metallic bookshelves are
individually attractive, but particularly
effective when used together.
www.presse-citron.com

Duo

Material Powder-coated steel
Dimensions 66 × 40 cm/
26 × 15¾ in.

The Duo shelf holds books securely
while giving the impression that
they are floating. Miami-born designer
Ana Linares is particularly intrigued
by origami and folded shapes inspired
by natural, organic forms. The height
of the shelf may vary.
www.analinaresdesign.com

Shadow

Material Stainless steel
Dimensions Various

||||||||||||||||||||||||||||||||||||||||||||||||||||||||||||

Mark Reigelman believes that wit is
an essential part of design, and describes
his bookshelves as 'assigning function
to shadows': the shadows suggest the kind
of shape the books they hold should cast.
www.markreigelman.com

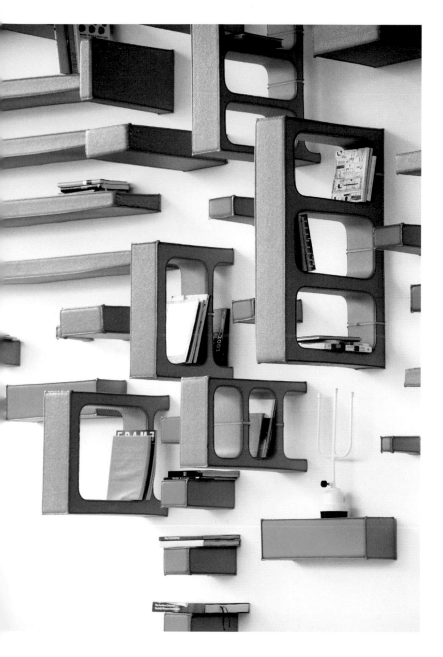

Melted Collection

Material Baked blue polystyrene
Dimensions Various
|||||||||||||||||||||||||||||||||||||||||||||||||||||||||||||||||||||||||||

These shelves are part of a collection
of blue furniture by Milan-based design
duo Pieke Bergmans and Peter van der
Jagt. The shapes are striking when seen
from a distance, but when examined
closely, the edges reveal themselves
to be melted and deformed.
www.piekebergmans.com

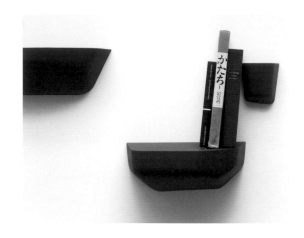

Roches >

Materials Fibreglass, dark anthracite
Dimensions Various

||||||||||||||||||||||||||||||||||||||||||||||||||||||||||||||||||||||||||||||||||||||||||||||||||||||||

These rock-like shelving units are available in eight sizes, ranging
from 13.5 to 117 cm (5 to 46 in.) long. A special ultra matte paint
gives them a velvety finish, and the shelf hides any fittings,
enhancing the organic look.

www.bouroullec.com

Quattro Line

Materials Coated aluminium, stainless steel
Dimensions 100 × 10 × 48 cm/ 39⅜ × 4 × 18⅞ in.
||||||||||||||||||||||||||||||||||||||||||||||||||||||||||||
Israeli designer Yedidia Blonder's Quattro Line pares the bookshelf down to its simplest form, and in doing so puts the books (which rest on both the shelf and wall) centre stage. The design comes in three sizes: Uno, Duo and Tre.
yedidia.blonder@gmail.com

< Fold

Material Steel
Dimensions 82 × 28 × 58 cm/ 32⅜ × 11 × 22¾ in.
||||||||||||||||||||||||||||||||||||||||||||||||||||||||||||
Fold by Angela and Mark Gilbert is made from a single sheet of steel, hand-folded into shape along laser-cut perforations – there are no joints or welds. The shape is inspired by the microscopic structures of plants, and works especially well when several are arranged together uniformly.
www.gilbert13.co.uk

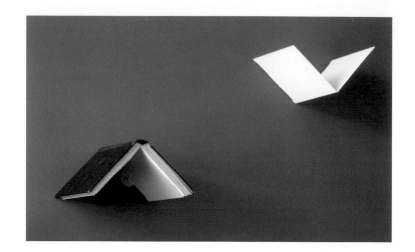

Flying Vee

Material Powder-coated sheet steel
Dimensions 22 × 11 × 16 cm
8¾ × 4¼ × 6¼ in.
||||||||||||||||||||||||||||||||||||||||||||||||||||||||||||||||
The components of the Flying Vee shelves
are available in a variety of colours, and
can be individually positioned to suit
the room. A single shelf can be set aside
for a favourite edition, or, alternatively,
a Vee could be hung upside down
to keep your place in a book.
www.massieoffice.com

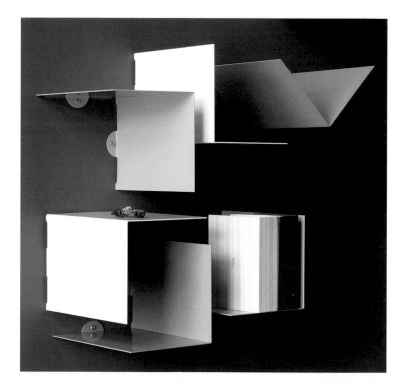

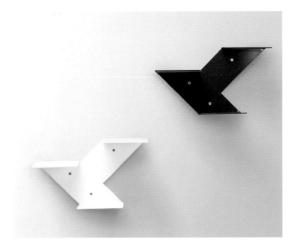

Fin

Material Painted steel

Dimensions 37 × 15 × 22 cm/
14⅜ × 5⅞ × 8¾ in.

||||||||||||||||||||||||||||||||||||||||||||||||||||||||||||||||||||||||||||||||||||

Depending on the arrangement, books placed on these shelves
can appear to be held in position by an invisible, gravity-defying
force. When mounted together, the units resemble a flock of birds
on the wing.

www.b-line.it

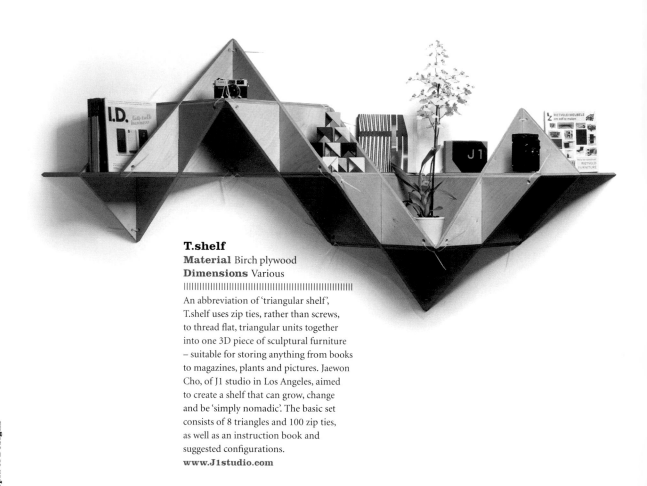

T.shelf
Material Birch plywood
Dimensions Various
||||||||||||||||||||||||||||||||||||||||||||||||||||||||||||||||||||||||

An abbreviation of 'triangular shelf',
T.shelf uses zip ties, rather than screws,
to thread flat, triangular units together
into one 3D piece of sculptural furniture
– suitable for storing anything from books
to magazines, plants and pictures. Jaewon
Cho, of J1 studio in Los Angeles, aimed
to create a shelf that can grow, change
and be 'simply nomadic'. The basic set
consists of 8 triangles and 100 zip ties,
as well as an instruction book and
suggested configurations.
www.J1studio.com

Readers Digest

Material Plywood
Dimensions 160 × 30 × 30 cm/
63 × 11⅞ × 11⅞ in.
|||||||||||||||||||||||||||||||||||||||||||||||||||||||||||||||||||
This design is part of the Ikea Hacks
project by Roman LindeBaum and
Rüdiger Otte. They use Ikea furniture to
examine the stereotypes and deficiencies
of mass production within 'a culture
affected by a flexibilization of work
and habitation, throwaway mentality
and lack of sensual experience'.
www.studioproxy.de

Rope Bridge Bookshelf

Materials Wood, paracord
Dimensions 79 × 28 cm/
31¼ × 11 in.
||||||||||||||||||||||||||||||||||||||||||||||||||||||||||||||||
'Most bookshelves require bookends
to keep the books up,' says Ed Lewis,
'but I thought that a more relaxed
approach would keep them all pushed
to the middle, thus the Rope Bridge
Bookshelf. This was made by taking
an Ekby Ståtlig shelf from Ikea, cutting
it into multiple pieces, drilling through
them, and then hanging them together
with paracord. Washers between
each piece of wood act as spacers.'
See how to build it at www.instructables.
com/id/Rope-Bridge-Bookshelf.
http://ed-lewis.com

Sinapsi

Material Lacquered polyurethane
Dimensions 130 × 21 × 60 cm/
51⅛ × 8¼ × 23⅝ in.
||||||||||||||||||||||||||||||||||||||||||||||||||||||||||||||||
Sebastian Errazuriz's Sinapsi is inspired
by neurons receiving electrical and
chemical impulses, a process he likens to
bookshelves receiving books and absorbing
them into their own environment. Sinapsi
also 'transmits' them via the branches
that extend along the wall.
www.horm.it

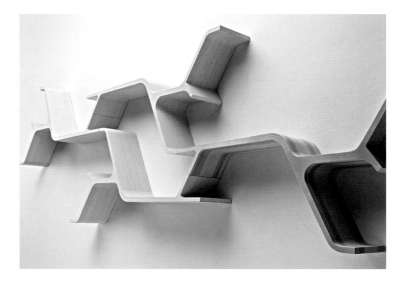

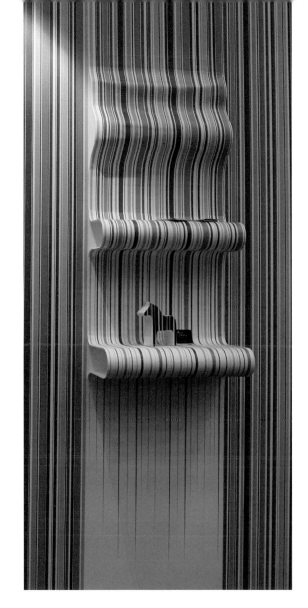

Off the Wall

Materials Wallpaper, acrylic sheets
Dimensions 45 × 250 cm/
17¾ × 98½ in.

||||||||||||||||||||||||||||||||||||||||||||||||||||||||||||||||||||||||||||||||||||||||||||||||||||||||||

This 3D wallpaper bulges out away from the wall to provide
a camouflaged bookshelf space. The wallpaper – which comes
in a range of patterns, including stripes and hoops – is printed
on demand by Swedish company Your Wallpaper.
www.kredema.se

Newton

Materials Mahogany, coated steel
Dimensions 80 × 18 × 13 cm/
31½ × 7 × 5⅛ in.
|||||||||||||||||||||||||||||||||||||||||||||||||||||||||||||||||||||||||
The perfect spot to keep your favourite
book, not so much shelved as suspended
in mid-air. The shelf is strong enough
to hold other books, if absolutely necessary.
www.studiove.com

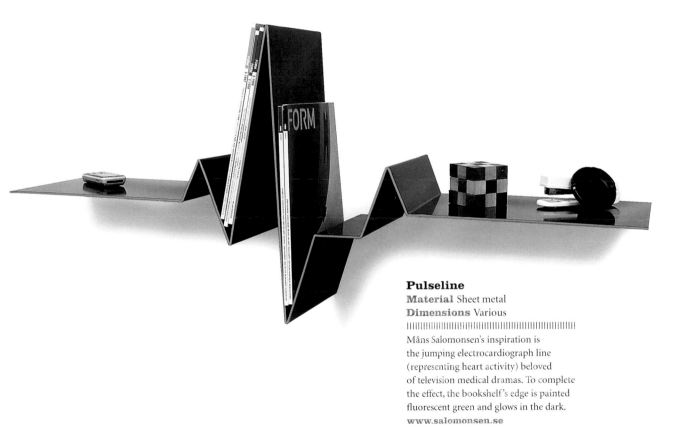

Pulseline

Material Sheet metal

Dimensions Various

Måns Salomonsen's inspiration is
the jumping electrocardiograph line
(representing heart activity) beloved
of television medical dramas. To complete
the effect, the bookshelf's edge is painted
fluorescent green and glows in the dark.
www.salomonsen.se

Single Shelves

Cantilever Bookshelf >
Materials Steel, concrete
Dimensions 180 × 25 cm/
70⅞ × 9¾ in.
|||||||||||||||||||||||||||||||||||||||||||||||||||||||||||
The height of Boston-based architect
Andrew Payne's bookshelf depends
on the weight of the books placed on it.
The slot in the middle of the shelf holds
an adjustable bookend that keeps the
volumes from toppling over.
www.liftarchitects.com

Piniwini
Material Brushed stainless steel
Dimensions Various
|||||||||||||||||||||||||||||||||||||||||||||||||||||||||||
Linus Svärm's design combines
a colourful peg with a hidden steel plate,
creating a shelf holding a pile of books
that appears to be perfectly –
if precariously – balanced.
www.karl-andersson.se

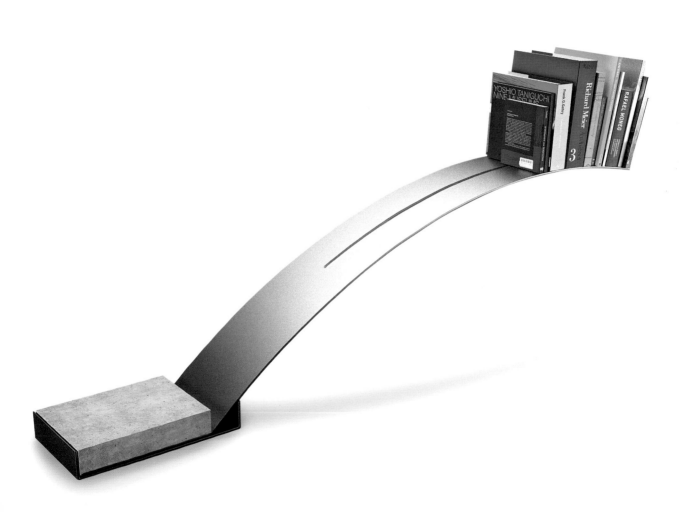

2

BOOKSHELF
FURNITURE

Since books are endlessly being picked up and put down around the home, it seems natural that designers should investigate combining shelving solutions and domestic furniture. The most common items to be given an inbuilt bookshelf are chairs and sofas, with shelves located in every conceivable area, from armrests to the actual bodies of the chairs themselves. Younes Duret's Ransa sofa (page 173), for example, gives the impression of levitating above a shelf of books. Tables also provide popular homes for shelf space, often within the legs of the construction. A perfect example is John Green's Embrace (page 166), a design that consists of two low tables made of laminated plywood, which may be interlocked to form a book storage unit and occasional table. Outside the sitting room, designers have begun to create den-like structures in which readers of all shapes, sizes and ages can relax, lounging *within* the bookcases themselves.

Those who live in small flats or apartments will know that space is at a premium, and that modern living does not always lie easily with large, cumbersome shelving units. When every square inch is valuable, it is often the dead space around baths, stairs and ceilings that can be usefully reclaimed. This desire to make the most out of space is one factor that has led to the present vogue for 'transformer furniture': objects that switch between multiple functions. Japanese designer Sakura Adachi's marvellous space-saving design Trick (page 170) can be a bookshelf one moment, and a table for two the next.

Tatik
Materials Plywood, paint, varnish
Dimensions 170 × 150 × 130 cm/
66⅞ × 59 × 51¼ in.
|||||||||||||||||||||||||||||||||||||||||||||||||||||||||||||||
A pyramidal bookshelf/chair with
volumes stored at angles. Designer
Tembolat Gugkaev, who works in
St Petersburg, says he likes the idea
of reading without getting up.
www.tembolat.com

< Bibliochaise
Materials Wood, leather
Dimensions 100 × 85 × 73 cm/
39⅜ × 33½ × 28¾ in.
|||||||||||||||||||||||||||||||||||||||||||||||||||||||||||||||
The Bibliochaise, designed by Giovanni
Gennari and Alisée Matta of the Milan
firm Nobody&co, contains 5 metres
(16 ft 3 in.) of shelf space, and comes
in white or black with leather cushions.
It has been used as part of the set for the
Sky Arts television programme *The Book
Show*, presented by Mariella Frostrup and
also appeared at the Charleston Trust's
Small Wonder short story festival.
www.nobodyandco.it

Fly

Materials Anodized extruded aluminium, stainless steel
Dimensions 27 × 9 × 190 cm/
10⅝ × 3⅝ × 74⅞ in.
||||||||||||||||||||||||||||||||||||||||||||||||||||||||||||||||||||||||||||||||||||
Fly is a bookshelf that incorporates a self-rolling projector
screen, which can easily be tucked out of sight when not needed.
The screen itself is 1.7 metres (5 ft 7 in.) wide.
www.matteoragni.com

Split Sink >

Material Corian
Dimensions 200 × 45 × 100 cm/
78¾ × 78¾ × 39⅜ in.
||||||||||||||||||||||||||||||||||||||||||||||||||||||||||||||||||||||||||||||||||||
Italian design company Emo regard the Split Sink as first of all
a piece of furniture and only then part of the plumbing. Ideal
for everybody who reads in the bath.
www.emo-design.it

Reading Lamp

Materials Polycarbonate, electronic
infrared switch, fluorescent light
Dimensions 25 × 10 × 18 cm/
9⅞ × 4 × 7 in.
||||||||||||||||||||||||||||||||||||||||||||||||||||||||||||||||||||||||||
This handy shelf doesn't just keep
your place in your book; it also has
an integrated light that turns on when
you take your book off, and off when
you put your book back on. Designed
by Alban Le Henry, Olivier Pigasse,
Vincent Vandenbrouck and
Jun Yasumoto, the Reading Lamp
is ideal for bedtime bookworms.
www.junyasumoto.com

Fiat Lux

Material Aluminium
Dimensions 18 × 18 × 27 cm/
7 × 7 × 10⅝ in.

|||||||||||||||||||||||||||||||||||||||||||||||||||||||||||||||||

A table lamp with a special section
in which a few select books can be stored.
When the lamp is turned on, the famous
phrase fiat lux ('let there be light')
appears on the side.
www.catenelson.com

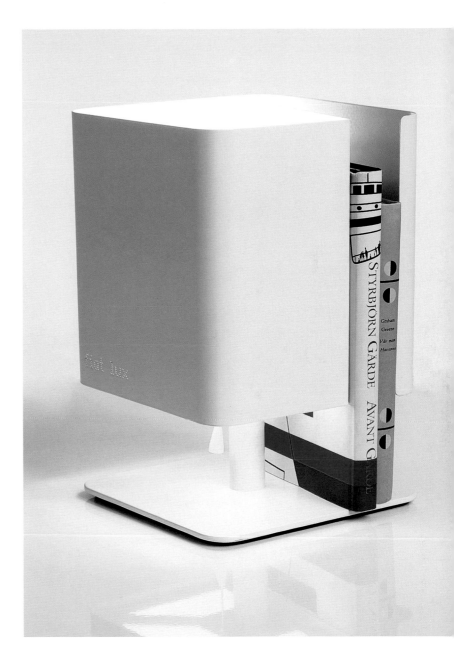

Ofo

Materials Unbuilt study

||||||||||||||||||||||||||||||||||||||||||||||||||||||||||||||||||||

A curvilinear design for a chair with integrated book storage by Maria and Igor Solovyov, who are based in Minsk.

www.solovyovdesign.by

Reading Hideaway

Materials Wood, metal, vinyl cushions
Dimensions 90 × 110 × 140 cm/
35½ × 43⅜ × 55¼ in.

||||||||||||||||||||||||||||||||||||||||||||||||||||||||||||||||||||||||||||

The Reading Hideaway is for use particularly in libraries,
schools and childrens' centres. Children can select a book
from the face-out display at each end, then curl up inside
to enjoy it. The Hideaway has a capacity of 132 paperbacks.

www.openingthebook.com

Powerlight

Materials Plywood, metal mesh, plaster
Dimensions 360 cm/
141 in. (diameter)
|||||||||||||||||||||||||||||||||||||||||||||||||||||||||||||||||||||||||||||||||||||||||||||
This bookcase, conference area and room divider is located
at the centre of photovoltaic specialists Powerlight Inc's office.
The outside is finished with Venetian plaster containing a golden
pigment that evokes the sun – fundamental to Powerlight's
business. Leger Wanaselja Architecture in California designed
the bookcase.
www.lwarc.com

Nautilus >

Materials Wood, laminated Shoji paper
Dimensions 120 × 170 cm/
47¼ × 66⅞ in.
|||||||||||||||||||||||||||||||||||||||||||||||||||||||||||||||||||||||||||||||||||||||||||||
Nautilus is a bookshelf with the potential for both linear and circular
arrangements. Alicia Bastian designed it as an heirloom object
to hold a family's favourite books; the rising shelves representing
the increase in age and knowledge as younger readers grow.
www.nmusalonesatellite.com

< Bookseat

Material Plywood
Dimensions 60 × 92 × 84 cm/
23⅝ × 36¼ × 33 in.
||||||||||||||||||||||||||||||||||||||||||||||||||||||||||||||||||||
According to its designer Mani Mani,
the pleasantly curvaceous Bookseat
is a 'creative design responding to
the advent of multifunctional spaces
in today's urban living'. It is available
with a felt or limited-edition leather
cushion.
www.bookseat.ca

Nook

Materials Maple hardwoods,
natural tung oil
Dimensions 110 × 96 × 38 cm/
43⅜ × 37⅞ × 14⅞ in.
||||||||||||||||||||||||||||||||||||||||||||||||||||||||||||||||||||
While wondering what would happen
if a bookshelf crashed into a coffee table,
Dave Pickett was inspired to create
the Nook. With an alcove for books,
the integrated piece of furniture gives
the impression – from some angles –
that it is floating.
www.david-pickett.com

Bookinist

Material Birch plywood
Dimensions 78 × 75 × 91 cm/
30¾ × 29½ × 35⅞ in.
||||||||||||||||||||||||||||||||||||||||||||||||||||||||||||
This bookchair/pushcart by Nils Holger
Moormann offers a comprehensive
reading experience: not only can it
hold around 80 paperbacks in the arms
and backrest, but it also sports a reading
lamp and hidden drawers for writing
equipment. A smaller version of the
Bookinist can be seen on page 244.
www.moormann.de

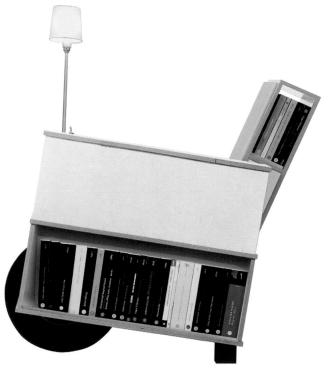

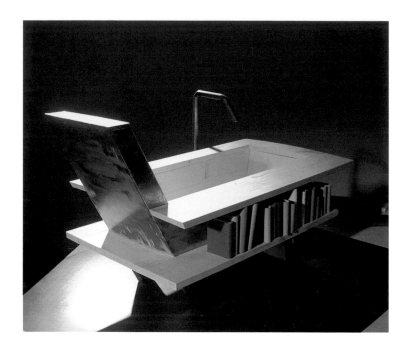

Library Bath
Materials Wood, stainless steel
Dimensions Various
||||||||||||||||||||||||||||||||||||||||||||||||||||||||||||||
A prototype hybrid of bath and
bookshelf. 'For me it is important
that a product is telling a story, and that
you get something more than its function
when you use or look at it,' says designer
Malin Lundmark, who lives and works
in Stockholm.
www.malinlundmark.com

Bookshelf Chair >
Materials Wood, metal frame
Dimensions 46 × 48 × 100 cm/
18⅛ × 18⅞ × 39⅜ in.
||||||||||||||||||||||||||||||||||||||||||||||||||||||||||||||
This bookcase, built in a square, maze-like
pattern, offers restricted storage space,
but ample opportunity to use spines
for decoration. The Bookshelf Chair
comes from Gadi Dudler, an industrial,
web and graphic designer from Israel.
www.gadidudler.carbonmade.com

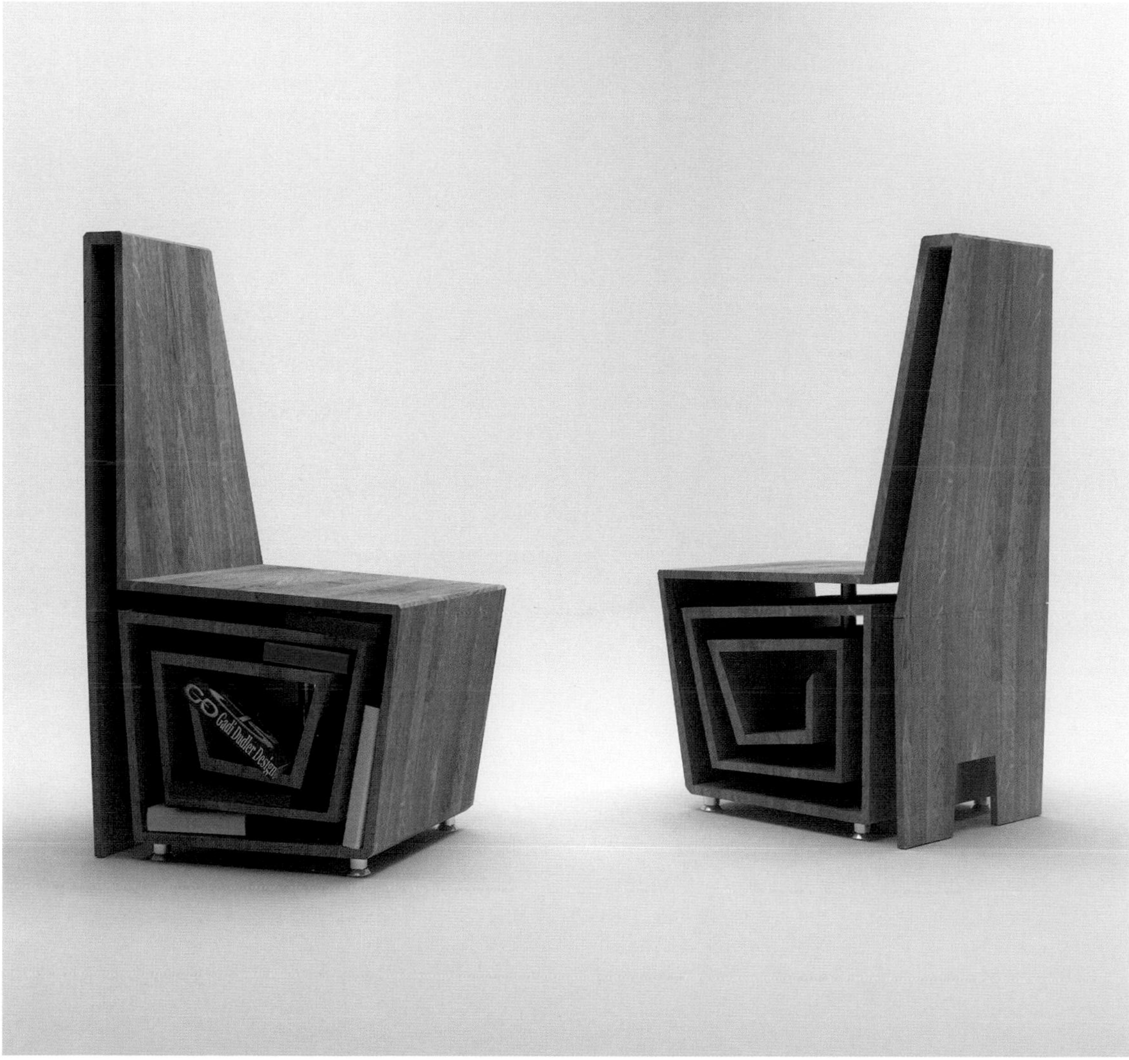
Gadi Dudler Design

Lili Lite >

Materials Wood, LED light
Dimensions 31 × 19 × 21 cm/
12⅛ × 7½ × 8¼ in.
||||||||||||||||||||||||||||||||||||||||||||||||||||||||||||
Lili Lite by Thijs Smeets from Amsterdam
is a reading light, bookmark and
bookshelf. Pick the book off the shelf
and a sensor turns on the LED light.
When you have finished, put it back
and out goes the light. There is also
an on/off switch if you prefer to
do it manually.
www.lililite.com

Reading Lamp

Materials Perspex, stainless steel
Dimensions 25 × 25 × 25 cm/
9⅞ × 9⅞ × 9⅞ in.
||||||||||||||||||||||||||||||||||||||||||||||||||||||||||||
A lamp, mini-bookshelf and magazine
stand in one – Reading Lamp has a built-in
slot for illuminating reads. The lamp
is designed by Hans van Veen and Floortje
Donia of Bureau de Bank, Utrecht.
www.bureaudebank.nl

Staircase
Material English oak

||||||||||||||||||||||||||||||||||||||||||||||||||||||||||||||||||||

Architects Levitate constructed this
staircase in a London flat, where space
limitations, coupled with the client's goal
of building a library, led to the creation
of an innovative library staircase that
holds around two thousand books.
The staircase was designed by structural
engineers Rodrigues Associates to transfer
the weight of the stairs and books back
to the main walls of the building. It
dangles from the upper floor, thereby
avoiding any complicated issues with
neighbours living below.
www.levitate.uk.com

Embrace
Materials Oak, birch or walnut veneer, birch plywood
Dimensions 85 × 35 × 38 cm/
33½ × 13¾ × 14⅞ in.
||||||||||||||||||||||||||||||||||||||||||||||||||||||||||||||||||||||||||||||||||||||||||
John Green's multifunctional bookcase furniture can be
configured to form two low tables, or (when the tables 'embrace')
a low bookcase and reading desk. The original brief was to develop
a modern variation on the classic Isokon Penguin Donkey design.
www.johngreendesigns.co.uk

Merdivan and Merduban >
Material Lacquered MDF
Dimensions 250 × 45 × 120 cm/
98½ × 17¾ × 47¼ in.
||||||||||||||||||||||||||||||||||||||||||||||||||||||||||||||||||||||||||||||||||||||||||||||||
Variations on stepladder shelving by Esra Sönmez Işlek, one model
featuring a bench and cushions within the structure. Additional
units can be added easily, and the rungs mean that shelves can
be set at differing heights.
www.labistanbul.com

Shelflife

Material Lacquered MDF
Dimensions 140 × 36 × 190 cm/
55⅛ × 14¼ × 74⅞ in.
||||||||||||||||||||||||||||||||||||||||||||||||||||||||||||||||||||||||||||||||||||||||||||||||||||||
A large bookshelf unit or room divider that includes
a chair and table within the structure to save space and clutter.
The London-based designer of Shelflife, Charles Trevelyan,
explains that 'Having noticed people browsing shelves with
an ever-growing pile of books under their arm as they balanced
another on top while skim-reading, it seemed that somewhere
to sit and read would be a useful addition.'
www.viablelondon.com

Broken Shelves

Materials Powder-coated steel, oiled MDF

Dimensions 90 × 200 × 30 cm/ 35½ × 78¾ × 11⅞ in.

||||||||||||||||||||||||||||||||||||||||||||||||||||||||||||||||||||||||

The 'broken' shelves provide an angled home for books in this flat-pack bookcase by Mareike Gast, from Frankfurt. Another unit in the same range includes a lamp, and functions as a reading den.

www.mareikegast.de

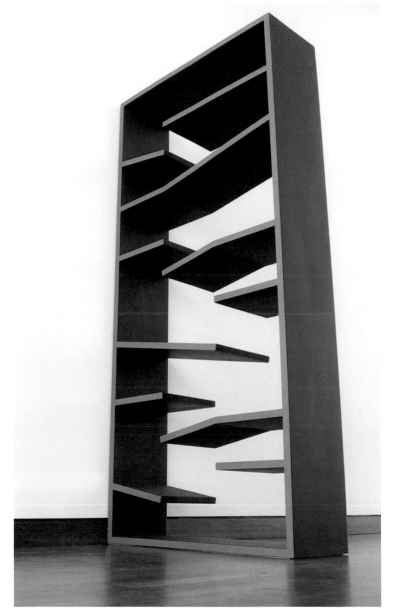

Trick

Materials Beech, birch, oak, ash, fabric
Dimensions 130 × 38 × 77 cm/ 51⅛ × 14⅞ × 30⅜ in.
||||||||||||||||||||||||||||||||||||||||||||||||||||||||||||||
A space-saving bookcase that can turn into a table and two chairs, all of which continue to hold books, even when the chairs are removed from the central table structure.
www.sakurah.net

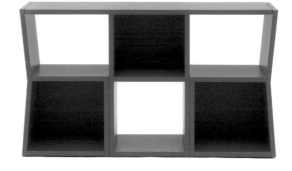

Cabinet Chair

Materials Powder-coated metal, wood

Dimensions 190 × 82 × 220 cm/ 74⅞ × 32¼ × 86⅝ in.

||||||||||||||||||||||||||||||||||||||||||||||||||||||||||||||||||

The first Cabinet Chair – its designers describe it as an 'information desk with a twist' – was created for a hotel lobby, allowing guests to peruse the shelves and giving them a handy spot in which to read. A monitor and keyboard have been added to this design.

www.ontwerpers.nu

Lost in Sofa
Materials Upholstered cubes
Dimensions 90 × 70 × 70 cm/
35½ × 27⅝ × 27⅝ in.
||||||||||||||||||||||||||||||||||||||||||||||||||||||||||||||||
Books can be 'shelved' between
the cushions of Tokyo designer Daisuke
Motogi's Lost in Sofa, which aims to make
the cracks between cushions useful, rather
than simply a limbo for loose change
and lost keys.
www.dskmtg.com

Compushelf

Material Injected plastic

Dimensions 150 × 35 × 25 cm/
59 × 13¾ × 9⅞ in.

|||||||||||||||||||||||||||||||||||||||||||||||||||||||

A bookshelf that incorporates a computer
and monitor – made with the multitasker
in mind. Shahaf Levavi also designed
Book Storage, which appears on page 267.

shahaf.levavi@gmail.com

Ransa

Material Wood

Dimensions 180 × 87 × 140 cm/
70⅞ × 34¼ × 55⅛ in.

|||||||||||||||||||||||||||||||||||||||||||||||||||||||||

Marrakech designer Younes Duret's
sofa appears to be hovering above the
integrated shelving below – an illusion that
works best when the shelves are fairly full.

www.younesdesign.com

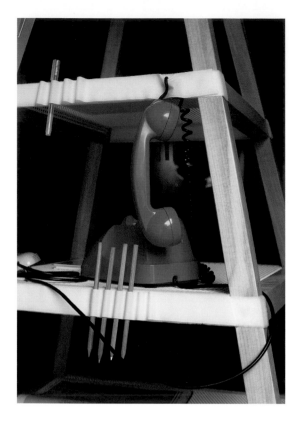

La Cultura Eleva

Materials Wood, perforated metal sheet, felt
Dimensions 90 × 100 × 220 cm/
35½ × 39⅜ × 86⅝ in.
||||||||||||||||||||||||||||||||||||||||||||||||||||||||||||||||||||||||||||||||||||||||||||||||||||||||||||||||||
Climb the 'Culture Elevates' bookcase to rise above it all
and read in style. Designed by Lilia Laghi and Mariano Pichler,
who describe it as a 'live-in bookshelf that messes with your usual
behaviour in the established domestic ritual that is reading …
It's a tower, a monument to the intellectual's quest for erudition!'
www.dotdotdot.it
www.plusdesigngallery.it

Forest

Materials Stainless steel and lacquer
fretwork, wood, gold leaf, mahogany
Dimensions 140 × 55 × 160 cm/
55⅛ × 21⅝ × 63 in.

|||||||||||||||||||||||||||||||||||||||||||||||||||||||||||||||

Inspired by the forms and functions
of nature, Forest aims to bring the
outdoors inside. The base is covered
in mahogany, while the interior is
decorated in gold leaf and a finish
of translucent orange, high-gloss varnish.
Designed and handcrafted by Boca
do Lobo in Rio Tinto, Portugal.
www.bocadolobo.com

Dondola
Material Stainless steel
Dimensions 52 × 83 × 130 cm/
20½ × 32¾ × 51¼ in.
||||||||||||||||||||||||||||||||||||||||||||||||||||||||||||||||||||
A particularly curvy rocking chair
designed by Pucci de Rossi, which also
features a useful book-storage area under
the seat. The books can be moved to alter
the balance of the Dondola: a filled front
section will keep it upright; while those
who prefer to read more horizontally
should store their books to the back.
www.made75.com

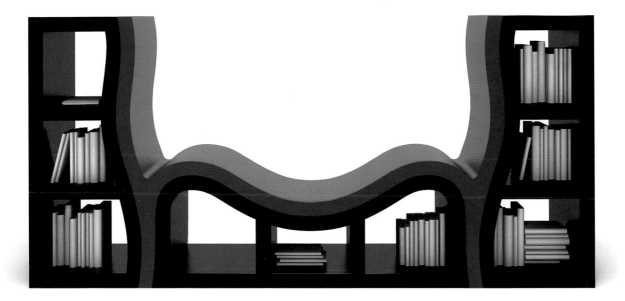

Console
Materials Painted MDF, polyurethane
Dimensions 210 × 50 × 110 cm/
82¾ × 19¾ × 43⅜ in.
||||||||||||||||||||||||||||||||||||||||||||||||||||||||||||||||||||||||||||||||||||||
Weighing 120 kg (265 lbs), the Console bench by Stanislav Katz
is a piece of baroque-inspired furniture that enables you to settle
down on the soft and springy polyurethane, bookended by your
own volumes.
www.katzhq.com

Snoop

Material Rotomoulded polyethylene
Dimensions 71 × 47 × 40 cm/
27⅞ × 18½ × 15¾ in.

|||||||||||||||||||||||||||||||||||||||||||||||||||||||||||||||||||||||||||||||||||||||||||||||||||||||||||

Designed by Karim Rashid, the Snoop has two built-in holders
for storing thinner books, and can be used as a stool or table.
The units – which come in white, yellow, topaz blue, pastel
green, basalt grey and red – can also be stacked to form
a standing bookcase.
www.b-line.it

Chin Up

Material Wood

Dimensions 90 × 40 × 80 cm/
35½ × 15¾ × 31½ in.

||||||||||||||||||||||||||||||||||||||||||||||||||||||||||||||||||||||||||||||||||||||||

Book spines are angled conveniently for browsing in Lisa Sandall's
freestanding Chin Up, which gives the impression that it's slipping
into the wall.

www.coroflot.com/lisasandall

2 / UNUSUAL BOOKSHELVES

While shops selling new and second-hand books face severe economic pressures, bookcase design is one aspect of book culture that seems to be flourishing. These remarkable constructions celebrate books, and use unusual features to put them centre stage in our lives.

One special design that illustrates how 'proper' bookshelves with a twist can enrich our lives is Bias of Thoughts (page 190) by John Leung of Australian architectural consultancy ClarkeHopkinsClarke. It was inspired by 2D drawings that appear to be 3D structures: look to the left of the bookcase and there appear to be four bookshelves, look to the right and there are just three. 'Visually,' Leung explains, 'the optical illusion serves as a reminder that, whenever one picks up a medium, ideas can be misinterpreted when passed from one end to the other.'

It's obvious that passion has been poured into these designs. Kittichai Reawsanguanwong's Chinese Chess Bookshelf (page 188) sprang from a lifetime's enjoyment of the game. He played it daily as a child and appreciated the Chinese characters on the pieces as much as the game itself. 'Why can't Chinese Chess be more popular internationally?' he asks. 'In the long run, I hope this will also communicate our Asian culture to non-Asian countries and increase the awareness of the Chinese Chess game.'

<<

Anatomy of a Murder
Materials Books, wood
Dimensions Various
||||||||||||||||||||||||||||||||||||||||||||||||||||||||||||||||||||||||||||||||||||||||||||||||
Jim Rosenau lives in California, where he turns unwanted
books into themed bookshelves. First he removes a portion
of the book's pages, replacing them with a frame of recycled
wood before attaching volumes together in appropriate groupings.
'I am interested in older hardback books that look better than
they read,' he says. 'I prefer books with strong type on the cover
and spine.'
www.thisintothat.com

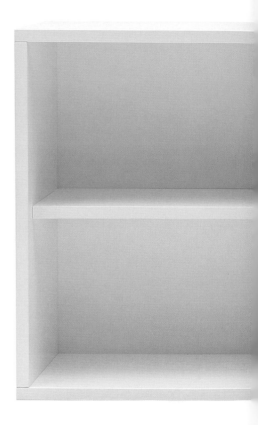

Pet Cave
Material Wood
Dimensions 160 × 40 × 72 cm/
63 × 15¾ × 28⅜ in.
||||||||||||||||||||||||||||||||||||||||||||||||||||||||||||||||||||||
'Animals' territorial behaviour is innate
and essential,' says Milan-based designer
Sakura Adachi. 'They always look for
a comfortable place to be in. Pet Cave
provides your pet (dog or cat) with such
a space. The pet house is surrounded by
shelves and comes with a little cushion
for them to rest on comfortably. It creates
a little space to encourage the relationship
between owner and pet.'
www.sakurah.net

Cable Car Book Cart

Materials Wooden book cart
Dimensions 120 × 35 × 130 cm/
47¼ × 13¾ × 51⅛ in.
||||||||||||||||||||||||||||||||||||||||||||||||||||||||||||||||||||
This customized book cart, built by
students and staff at Gleeson Library,
University of San Francisco, was the
winning entry in the 2010 Pimp My
Bookcart competition (run by the
library-themed comic strip *Unshelved*).
The cart was built in homage to
San Francisco's iconic cable cars.
Note the roof-mounted bronze desk bell.
www.usfca.edu/Library

Book Bike

Materials Bicycle, wood
Dimensions Various
||||||||||||||||||||||||||||||||||||||||||||||||||||||||||||||||||||
Since 2008, Gabriel Levinson has been
handing out thousands of free books
across Chicago from his custom-built
tricycle and mobile bookcase. 'Everyone
has the right to build and cherish a private
library,' says Levinson, who obtains all his
volumes from independent bookshops
using public donations to his website.
www.bookbike.org

Bike Shelf

Material Walnut or ash
Dimensions 44 × 13 × 40 cm/
17¼ × 5⅛ × 15¾ in.
||||||||||||||||||||||||||||||||||||||||||||||||||||||
Chris Brigham, another creative San
Franciscan, designed the Bike Shelf to fill
what he saw as a 'void in elegant bike
management'. The top tube is held by an
attractive shelf, which keeps both bike and
books close to hand, yet out of the way.
www.theknifeandsaw.com

Unusual Bookshelves

Cat-Library
Material Birch plywood
Dimensions 38 cm²/
14⅞ in.² (per cube)
||||||||||||||||||||||||||||||||||||||||||||||||||||||||||||||||||||||
Specially designed for shelf-stalking
cats, Corentin Dombrecht's Cat-Library
modules are neither painted nor oiled
to prevent paws slipping on the stairs.
The stairway can be hidden away at the
back of the shelf, giving cats a secret
passage behind the books.
www.corentin.be

Walking Bookcase

Materials Oak, stainless steel
Dimensions 140 × 89 × 120 cm/
55⅛ × 35 × 47¼ in.

|||||||||||||||||||||||||||||||||||||||||||||||||||||||||||||||||||

Wouter Scheublin's design is inspired
by the walking platform invented by
19th-century Russian mathematician
Pafnuty Chebyshev. When the machine
is pushed the legs 'walk' using a system
of cranks and rods, 'perplexing our
perception of the ordinarily static piece
of furniture', as Scheublin describes it.
The Walking Bookshelf was chosen by
Wallpaper* magazine to house their City
Guides series at the 2010 'Handmade …
in Italy' exhibition.

www.wouterscheublin.com

Unusual Bookshelves

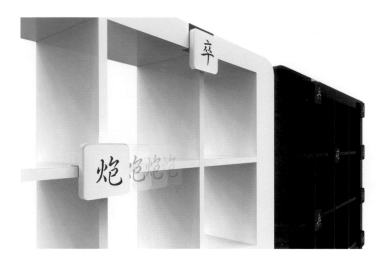

The Chinese Chess Bookshelf

Materials Wood, ceramic, magnets
Dimensions 200 × 20 × 180 cm/
78¾ × 7⅞ × 70⅞ in.

||||||||||||||||||||||||||||||||||||||||||||||||||||||||||||||||||||||||||

Not only can you store your books
on these shelves, but you can also play
Xiangqi (Chinese chess), in which the
pieces move along lines, rather than
between squares. Magnets on the back
of the pieces hold them in place on the
joints, allowing players to stop or resume
games at leisure. 'I want to bring this
game that I always loved into our daily
lives, so that it can reach more people,'
says designer Kittichai Reawsanguanwong.
www.sketch-d.com

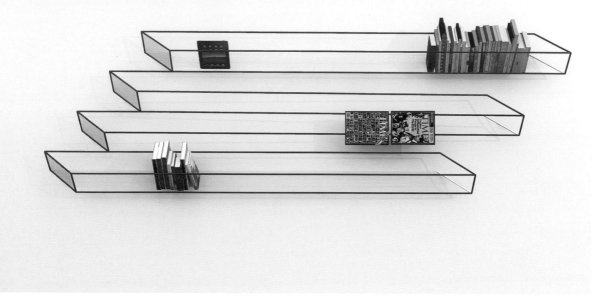

Bias of Thoughts

Materials Acrylic, aluminium frame
Dimensions 300 × 120 × 25 cm/
118 × 47¼ × 9¾ in.

||||||||||||||||||||||||||||||||||||||||||||||||||||||||||||||||||

This bookshelf is a 3D structure inspired
by a 2D optical illusion drawing – pass
your eyes from one side to the other
to get the full effect. As well as storage,
the aluminium frame of Bias of Thoughts
makes an ideal place to hang magazines.
www.john-leung.com

Primer B

Materials Polymethyl methacrylate,
stainless steel

Dimensions 150 × 30 × 27 cm/
59 × 11⅞ × 10⅝ in.

||||||||||||||||||||||||||||||||||||||||||||||||||||||||||||||||

A letter box that acts as a communal
bookshelf to encourage neighbours
get to know each other better by swapping
books. There are two parts: a transparent
section to showcase available books,
and a secure one into which the requested
books can be dropped for exchange.
But if you want a book, you have to
visit your neighbour and ask for it …

www.joanrojeski.com

2

/ BOOKSHELVES AS ART

Books are marvellous raw materials for artists: Nina Katchadourian's Sorted Books project coordinates spines to tell short stories, Chris Cobb arranged the books in San Francisco's Adobe Bookstore by colour, and Mike Stilkey in California actually paints pictures on stacks of books. Sculptor Livio de Marchi has even built a wooden house in which all the furniture appears to have been made from of books. Nicholson Baker's playful essay 'Books As Furniture' for the *New Yorker* magazine analyses how books – and imitation books – are used as props to create atmosphere in mail order catalogue photographs.

But the bookshelves and bookcases on which the books sit also inspire artists to play with various ideas, from gravity and perspective to religion and the very place of knowledge within our society. These conceptual bookshelves can be as domestic as wallpaper prints or *trompe l'œil* painted walls, but often say something about the nature of reading. Niko Economidis's Read-Unread Bookshelf (page 201) is built using a leather strap that hangs across supports and literally weighs on one side a pile of books that have already been read against books yet to be started on the other.

Bookshelf designs can also be monumental, such as Sanja Medic's ceramic-and-brick construction in Lootsstraat, Amsterdam (page 196): this situates 250 book spines, each bearing the title of a poem, in a neighbourhood where streets are named after 18th- and 19th-century Dutch poets and writers.

The Community Bookshelf in downtown Kansas City, Missouri, is an example of book art on a vast scale. Twenty-two book spines made from signboard mylar run along the south wall of the Central Library's parking garage, together creating a 'shelf' that stands 7.6 metres (25 ft) tall. The titles were suggested by Kansas City readers and then selected by the Kansas City Public Library Board of Trustees.

<<
Alasdair Macintyre
Materials Oil on canvas
Dimensions 65 × 74 cm/
25⅜ × 29⅛ in.
||||||||||||||||||||||||||||||||||||||||||||||||||||||||||||||
Alasdair Macintyre (2008) is one of a series
of portraits of people as seen through
their bookshelves. See page 199 for
more of Victoria Reichelt's work.
www.victoriareichelt.com

Vintage Bookshelf
Wallpaper
Material Textured coloured paper
Dimensions 55 × 300 cm/
21⅜ × 118⅛ in.
||||||||||||||||||||||||||||||||||||||||||||||||||||||||||||||
Designed by Young & Battaglia and
made in England, the wallpaper recreates
the look of a vintage library filled
with shelves of old books. An alternative
version with white books on white shelves
is also available.
www.studiomold.com

De Batavier (De Boekenkast)
Materials Ceramic, brick
Dimensions 750 × 250 cm/
295 × 98 in.
||||||||||||||||||||||||||||||||||||||||||||||||||||||||||||||||||||||||||||||||||||||||||||||||||||||
Sanja Medic designed this façade for a building in Lootsstraat,
Amsterdam – an area where the streets are named after Dutch
poets and writers from the 18th and 19th centuries. The frontage
is a boekenkast ('bookcase') of 250 ceramic spines, and the titles
are taken from the works of the authors commemorated by the
local street names.
www.sanjamedic.com

Boox

Material Cardboard

Dimensions 17 × 20 × 25 cm/
6¾ × 7⅞ × 9¾ in.

|||||||||||||||||||||||||||||||||||||||||||||||||||||||||||||||||||||||||||||||||||||||||||||||

Storage boxes decorated with fictional book spines (including such titles as *The Neverending Storage*). Created by Shahar Peleg, whose studio – Peleg Design – is in Tel Aviv.

www.peleg-design.com

Layers Book Chair

Materials Books, steel
Dimensions 100 × 80 × 80 cm/
39⅜ × 31½ × 31½ in.

||||||||||||||||||||||||||||||||||||||||||||||||||||||||||||||||||||||||||||||||||||

This chair, produced as part of Richard Hutten's Layers furniture series, is built up in levels: a plea for more depth in the design world. 'A book is all about layers of meaning,' says Hutten.
www.richardhutten.com

< Yellow Fever, Orange County

Materials Oil on canvas
Dimensions 81 × 81 cm/
31⅞ × 31⅞ in.

|||||||||||||||||||||||||||||||||||||||||||||||||||||||

Inspired partly by the work of Mondrian, Queensland artist Victoria Reichelt paints bookshelves according to theme and colour, rather than the literary significance of the contents. The bookshelf becomes an image separate from its texts, yet still attractive for what it represents.
www.victoriareichelt.com

Bookshelves as Art

Read-Unread

Materials Leather, chrome-plated rods
Dimensions 390 × 4 cm/
153⅜ × 1⅝ in.
||||||||||||||||||||||||||||||||||||||||||||||||||||||||||||||||||||||||||||
Read-Unread is built using leather straps
hung across wall-mounted supports.
The design literally weighs your books,
comparing those already read against those
still to be consumed. Niko Economidis also
designed the Director bookcase (page 76).
www.nikoeconomidis.com

Bookshelf Dress
Material Silk charmeuse
Dimensions Below knee length
||||||||||||||||||||||||||||||||||||||||||||||||||||||||||
Chilean-born designer Maria Cornejo's
Bookshelf Dress, inspired by the library
of one of her friends, was one of the
major attractions of the Zero + Maria
Cornejo fall/winter 2011 collection.
www.zeromariacornejo.com

Crisis
Material Wood
Dimensions 120 × 32 × 140 cm/
47¼ × 12⅜ × 55⅛ in.
||||||||||||||||||||||||||||||||||||||||||||||||||||||||||||||||||||||||||||||||||||||||||||||||||
The shelves of Crisis feature an assortment of permanent objects
that represent what we value in society, as well as our needs and
our worries.
www.catenelson.com

D'Espresso
Material Printed tiles
Dimensions 39 m²/
420 ft²
||||||||||||||||||||||||||||||||||||||||||||||||||||||||||||||||||||||||||||||||||||||||||||||||||||||||||||||||||
Nemaworkshop designed the interior of this espresso bar on
Madison Avenue, New York, using a bookcase-turned-on-its-side
theme. The book-lined 'shelves' (sepia-toned full-size photographs
of books, printed on custom tiles) become the floor, wall and ceiling.
www.nemaworkshop.com

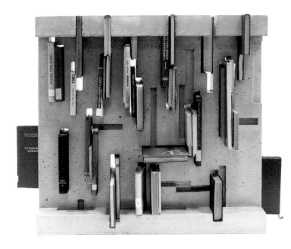

Hübler Applied Literature
Materials Concrete, glass
Dimensions Various

The gaps in the podium of this bookshelf table are filled with politically outdated volumes donated by the Research Institute Library of Radio Free Europe, a broadcaster that opposed communism before the collapse of the Soviet Union. 'The table constitutes a monument to … the degeneration of information, to the immortality of the past and to its disintegration,' says Hungarian artist János Hübler.
www.ivanka.hu
www.hublerjanos.com

< Ruined Bookshelf
Material Bronze
Dimensions 150 × 60 × 230 cm/
59 × 23⅝ × 90⅝ in.

New York artist Jude Tallichet's sculpture is a replica of the bookshelf that collapsed in her apartment. She describes her sculpture, installed in a vacant site in Miami, Florida, as an 'acropolis of gorgeous ruin'. The work represents the catastrophic loss of harmony that results from natural and manmade disasters, as well as the information age's alteration of the social order.
http://judetallichetstudio.com

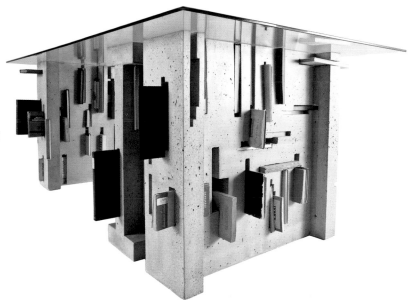

Bibliotheque Outlandia

Materials Wood, ink
Dimensions Various

||||||||||||||||||||||||||||||||||||||||||||||||||||||||||||||||||||||||||||||||||||||||||||||||||||||||||||||||||||||||

Outlandia is a *trompe l'œil* library, installed in a self-sufficient tree house and artist's studio in Glen Nevis, Lochaber, Scotland. Artist Adam Dant has transformed the interior into a place for the 'categorization of knowledge and observations' in the style of the 18th-century Scottish Enlightenment – visitors can write their own titles on to the spines of the books.

www.outlandia.com

Bookshelves as Art

2

/ OUTSIDE THE BOX

While the vast majority of bookshelves in homes around the world are built to a standard box design with horizontal planking, there is no reason why readers should not populate their rooms with more intriguingly shaped bookcases. Billy's Brother (page 218) from Addi is a typical example of a more fluid, wave-like approach, inspired by a collection of sketches of the Berlin and New York skylines. The shape of Billy's Brother can be repeated and the different parts fitted together to form a long sculpture against a wall or to serve as a room divider.

Shelves need not be static, either. Rotating bookshelves in particular have a long history. One of the many ingenious devices at the Monticello home of Thomas Jefferson (co-author of the Declaration of Independence) is his revolving bookstand, which can hold five books at adjustable angles on rests that fold down to form a cube (it is now possible to buy a reproduction of the original, made of solid mahogany). Among the modern takes on interactive bookshelves is Patatras (page 226) by Michaël Bihain. This large wheel has slots to hold books, and can roll around the room even when fully laden.

Perhaps as a result of increasing environmental awareness, there are also many varieties of tree-shaped shelves available, their 'branches' providing convenient rests for books. Other shelves take the form of clouds, punctuation marks and electric circuits, and there are even bookcases shaped like cows, polar bears or dogs. The shelves themselves can also be re-imagined: Kwan (page 226) by Dutch designers Studio Ditte replaces shelves with rods, inspired by the way laundry in China is dried on horizontal sticks hanging from the window.

<<
Sherman Contemporary Art Foundation
Bibliotheca (detail)
Materials Transparent acrylic,
LED lights
Dimensions 50 m²/
540 ft²

|||||||||||||||||||||||||||||||||||||||||||||||||||||||||||||||||||||||||||||||||

This architectural installation was commissioned to display
books and catalogues during the first anniversary of the SCAF
in Sydney. The shelves are honeycomb-shaped cells, backlit using
energy-efficient LED lights.

www.l-a-v-a.net

Flamingo >
Materials Plexiglas, wood
Dimensions 130 × 35 × 160 cm/
51¼ × 13¾ × 63 in.

|||||||||||||||||||||||||||||||||||||||||||||||||||||||||||||||||||||||||||||||||

Inspired by the famous stance of the eponymous bird, the various
elements of Flamingo support one another due to the force of
gravity – having more books on the shelves increases stability.
Mist-o is a Milan-based design partnership between Tommaso
Nani and Noa Ikeuchi, who say Flamingo is based on the principle
of reduction to the essential.

www.mist-o.com

See-Saw
Material American walnut
Dimensions 25 × 220 × 50 cm/
9⅞ × 86⅝ × 19¾ in.

|||||||||||||||||||||||||||||||||||||||||||||||||||||||||||||||||||||||||||||||||||

How do you weigh the importance of a book? 'By playing
with balance, the See-Saw bookshelf visualizes the breadth
of our home libraries,' say designers Boaz Cohen and Sayaka
Yamamoto. 'Is Kafka truly heavier than the latest issue of *Vogue*?'

www.bexsy.com

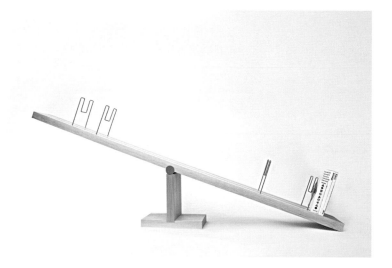

Archive

Material Wood
Dimensions Various

||||||||||||||||||||||||||||||||||||||||||||||||||||||||||||||||||||||||||||||||||||||||||||||||||||

The Archive series from Danish design studio David Garcia examines the physical weight of information, and the relationship between books and humans. Archive I (opposite) features a reading chair, elevated according to the weight of volumes in the bookcase. Archive II (below and opposite) is a circular, nomadic library in which the reader can travel with their own books.
www.davidgarciastudio.com

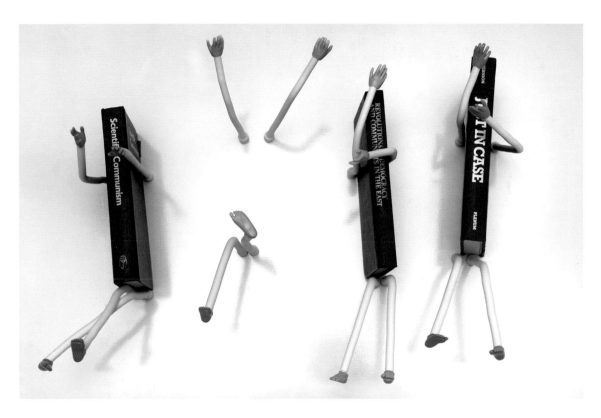

< Spring Roll
Materials Aluminium, fabric
Dimensions Various
||||||||||||||||||||||||||||||||||||||||||||||||||||||||
Fabric snakes around rods on a stand
to form ad hoc cradles for books in
Alessandro De Dominicis's labyrinthine
Springroll design.
www.coroflot.com/dedo

Movement Bookcase
Materials Nails, wood
Dimensions Various
||||||||||||||||||||||||||||||||||||||||||||||||||||||||
A bookcase with genuine character: bent
nails affixed with dolls' hands and feet
are used to bring books to life. Designer
Wonsuk Cho also created the Hanger
bookshelf (page 243).
www.samulnoli.com

Billy's Brother
Material MDF
Dimensions 200 × 90 × 170 cm/
78¼ × 35½ × 66⅞ in.
||||||||||||||||||||||||||||||||||||||||||||||||||||||||||||||||||||||||||||||||||||||||||||||||||||
Billy's Brother is a wave-like bookcase and sculpture inspired by
the skylines of Berlin and New York. In places the bookshelf twists
laterally, giving the impression that the books might fall off. Billy's
Brother comes flat packed, and can be put together in minutes.
www.addi.se

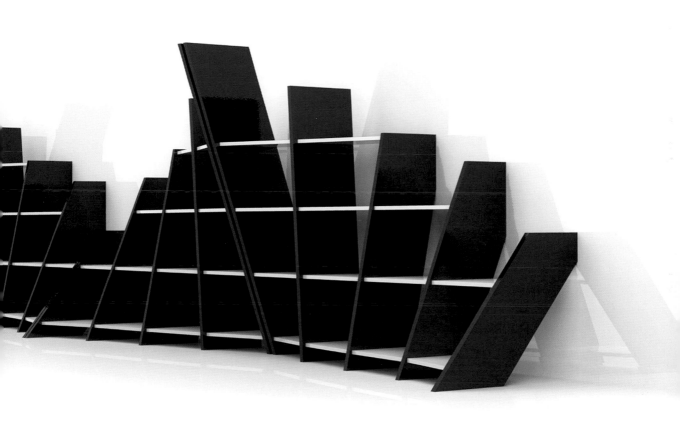

< Booksling

Materials Elastic sheet, wooden poles
Dimensions Various

||||||||||||||||||||||||||||||||||||||||||||||||||||||||||

The aim of Booksling is to create
a shelving system that only takes up as
much space as is needed. A book put on
the shelf causes it to stretch and transform
its size and shape – it is, as designer Tolga
Soran says, 'a reminder of what books
really are: a heavy load of information,
feelings and expressions.'
www.coroflot.com/tsoran

Stretch Shelf

Materials Cast rubber, machined
anodized aluminum
Dimensions 25 cm/
9⅞ in. (diameter)

||||||||||||||||||||||||||||||||||||||||||||||||||||||||||

Pete Oyler describes his Stretch Shelf as
'essentially a giant rubber band' hooked
around short aluminium posts – a simple
bookshelf, but visually appealing enough
to bring a smile to any readers' face.
www.peteoyler.com

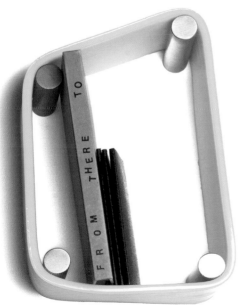

Library Head

Material Wood
Dimensions 180 × 150 × 240 cm/
70⅞ × 59 × 94½ in.
||||||||||||||||||||||||||||||||||||||||||||||||||||||||||||||||||
The Library Head was designed by
conceptual artist Nicola Lanzenberg
in 1989 (the bicentenary of the French
Revolution, with its many beheadings).
'My head is a library,' she says,
'this library is my head.'
www.nicolal.com

Osisu Elephant (right)
Materials Reclaimed teak and sawdust
Dimensions Various
||||||||||||||||||||||||||||||||||||||||||||||||||||||||||||||||||
Thai design company Osisu produces
handmade objects from waste material
that has been found at construction sites,
or thrown away during manufacturing
processes. The materials used range from
reclaimed teak, sawdust and food
packaging to salvaged ventilation grills.

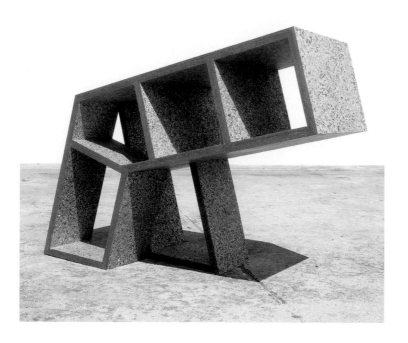

Osisu Humpback

Material Reclaimed food packaging
Dimensions Various
||||||||||||||||||||||||||||||||||||||||||||||||||||||||||||||||||||||
Using these reclaimed and recycled
materials, Singh Intrachooto has designed
a series of largely animal-inspired
bookshelves, including: Elephant
(previous page); Baby Elephant; Boar;
Giraffe; Humpback (left); Stan; and Sway.

Pack of Dogs 2

Material Ceramic
Dimensions 51 × 29 × 17 cm/
20 × 11½ × 6¾ in.

||||||||||||||||||||||||||||||||||||||||||||||||||||||||||||||||||||||||||||||||||||||||||||||

A low bookshelf inspired by the shape of a small dog.
The traditionally manufactured pieces are named after famous
Mexican wrestlers – Dos Caras Jr, Aguayo, Superastro, El Santo,
Alushe and Místico. Pack of Dogs 2 was created by NEL, the same
collective that designed the Torres de Satélite bookshelf (page 65).

www.nel.com.mx

Patatras

Material Expanded polypropylene
Dimensions 120 cm/
47¼ in. (diameter)
||||||||||||||||||||||||||||||||||||||||||||||||||||||||||||||
These colourful rolling bookshelves 'could
be interpreted as a wheel of knowledge,'
says designer Michaël Bihain (who also
created Libri on page 24). Fifteen single
volumes can be shelved in the storage
cells and, if you're feeling brave, Patatras
can be stacked.
www.bihain.com

Kwan >

Material Spray-painted MDF
Dimensions 140 × 25 × 140 cm/
55¼ × 9⅞ × 55¼ in.
|||||||||||||||||||||||||||||||||||||||||||||||||||||||||||||||||||||||||||||||||||||||
A practically shelfless bookcase, Kwan (Chinese for 'stick')
is inspired by the way laundry is dried in China on horizontal
batons protruding from windows.
www.studioditte.nl

Joe and Joe Junior

Material Laminated wood
Dimensions Various

||||||||||||||||||||||||||||||||||||||||||||||||||||||||||||||||||||||||||||||||||||||||||||||||||

A talking-point bookshelf, Joe (below) is an 80-kg (176-lb) polar bear whose body is completed as the shelves are filled up. There is a special website charting the location of every one of the 50 Joes around the world (www.joethepolarbear.com). Designer Benoît Convers has also created a smaller Joe Junior (left).
www.ibride.fr

Estante Vaco
Material Wood
Dimensions Various
||||||||||||||||||||||||||||||||||||||||||||||||||||||||||||||||||||||||||||||||||||||||||||
Designer Dennys Tormen won first prize in the inaugural Brazilian
Sustainable Design Competition with his cow-shaped bookcase: all
materials were sourced from a cooperative that turns waste paper
into a hard, plate-like material.
www.dennystormen.com

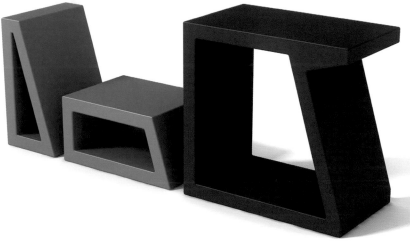

Mellow

Material Rotomoulded plastic
Dimensions Various

||||||||||||||||||||||||||||||||||||||||||||||||||||||||||||||

'The idea is to establish a relationship between the convenient and the playful,' say designers Helena Bueno and Heinz Müller from Baíta Design. 'Mellow is great for home, a kid's room or to add some life to a boring office.' All the modules can be moved or removed to suit their space and use – or if you simply want to play with the shapes and colours.

www.baitadesign.com

Tree Bookshelf >

Material Powder-coated steel
Dimensions 150 × 20 × 210 cm/ 59 × 7⅞ × 82¾ in.

||||||||||||||||||||||||||||||||||||||||||||||||||||||||||||||||||

'A tree becomes a book becomes a tree,' says designer Shawn Soh, whose design was inspired by childhood memories of sticking letters on tree branches. 'Books become flowers of the tree, and part of the artwork itself in its day-to-day use.' Made from metal instead of wood to save trees.

www.designartist.co.kr

Tree Shelves

Material Wood

Dimensions 180 × 30 × 200 cm/
70⅞ × 11¾ × 78¾ in.

||||||||||||||||||||||||||||||||||||||||||||||||||||||||||||||||||||||||||||||

A bookcase that looks at once both
organic and geometric, Tree Shelves
is specifically designed by Vadim
Kibardin to house those books about
design, art and architecture that come
in unusual sizes, and can often be hard
to fit on ordinary shelves. The design is
available with a transparent lacquer,
japan black or cherry finish.
www.kibardindesign.com

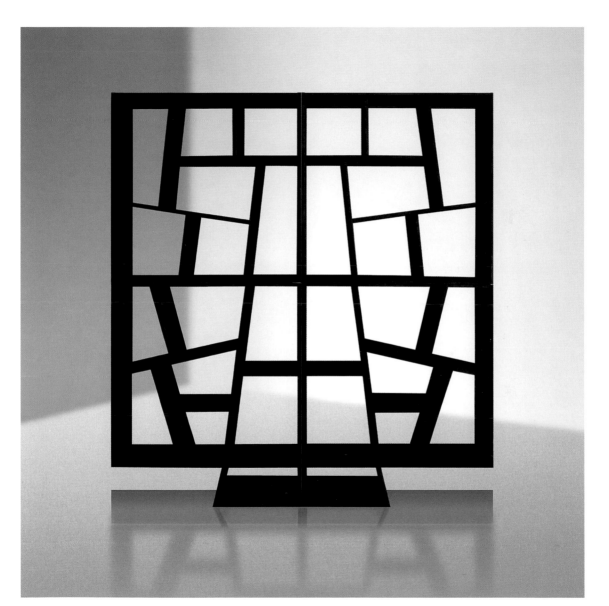

Branch Bookshelf
Materials Oak or walnut veneer, plywood
Dimensions 320 × 25 × 220 cm/ 125 × 9⅞ × 86⅜ in.
||||||||||||||||||||||||||||||||||||||||||||||||||||||||||||||||||||||
Trunkless branches radiate attractively across the room, providing plenty of storage space for books. Smaller shoots form natural bookends.
www.olivier-dolle.com

Bookwave
Materials Felt, stainless steel
Dimensions 60 × 20 × 220 cm/
23⅜ × 7⅞ × 86⅝ in.
||||||||||||||||||||||||||||||||||||||||||||||||||||||||||||||||||||||
A bookshelf. And a curtain. This cradle for
books protects each individual volume,
though the arrangement of spines and
covers means that looking for specific titles
is not always a swift process. Bookwave was
created by Mehtap Obuz, a director at
Istanbul-based Demirden Design.
www.demirden.com

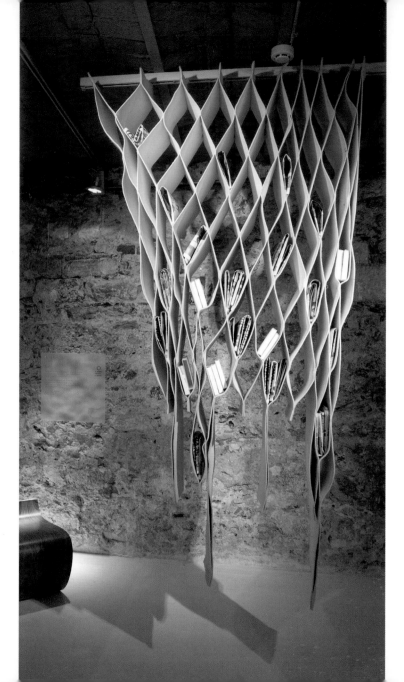

238

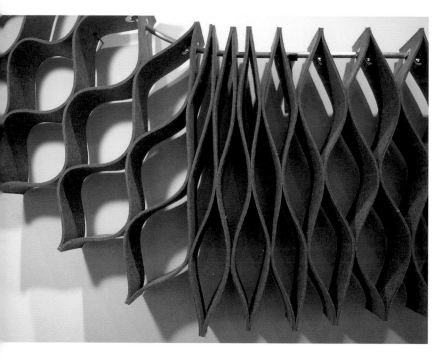

A Cornucopia of Designs

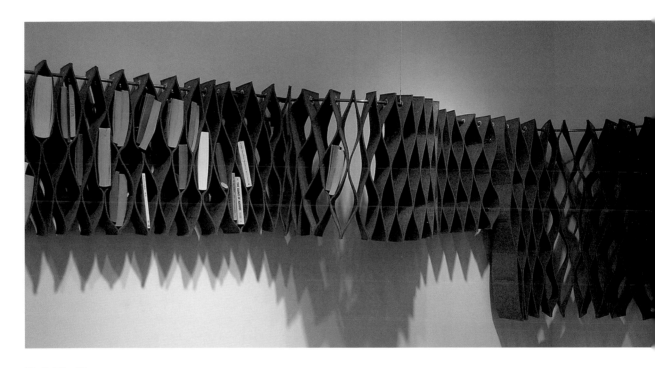

Soft Shelf

Materials Velcro, industrial-grade felt, stainless steel
Dimensions Various
||||||||||||||||||||||||||||||||||||||||||||||||||||||||||||||||||||||||||||||||||||||||||||||||||||
This concertina bookshelf can expand or contract, depending on
the space available or the number of books kept inside. The felt is
cut into vertical strips and stitched at intervals to create pockets, and
the units are hung like curtains from aluminium eyelets on a rod.
www.lateralarch.com

Softwall >
Materials Felt
Dimensions 200 × 16 × 190 cm/
78¾ × 6¼ × 74⅞ in.
||||||||||||||||||||||||||||||||||||||||||||||||||||||||||||||||||||
As much a room divider as a bookcase,
Softwall is the perfect place to slot titles
in at random. The design, by Carsten
Gerhards and Andreas Glucker, means your
current reading choices can be seen, and
accessed, from both sides of the bookcase.
www.bebitalia.com

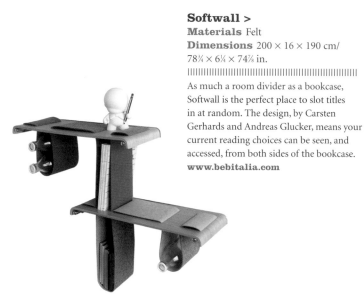

Boa
Materials Beech or oak, felt
Dimensions 45 × 14 cm/
17¾ × 5½ in. (height various)
||||||||||||||||||||||||||||||||||||||||||||||||||||||||||||||||||||
The Boa by Norwegian designers
Margarita Garcia and Pål Jacobsen can
be used as a single shelf, but its modular
formation provides the flexibility to build
an interconnecting bookshelf system. The
felt also creates the locking mechanism
between the wooden shelf and the
mounting bracket.
www.tuyodesign.no

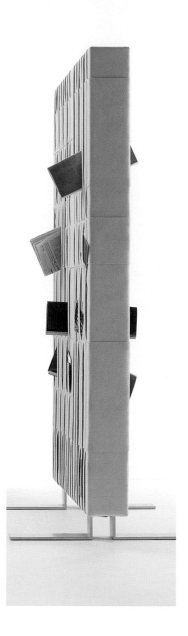

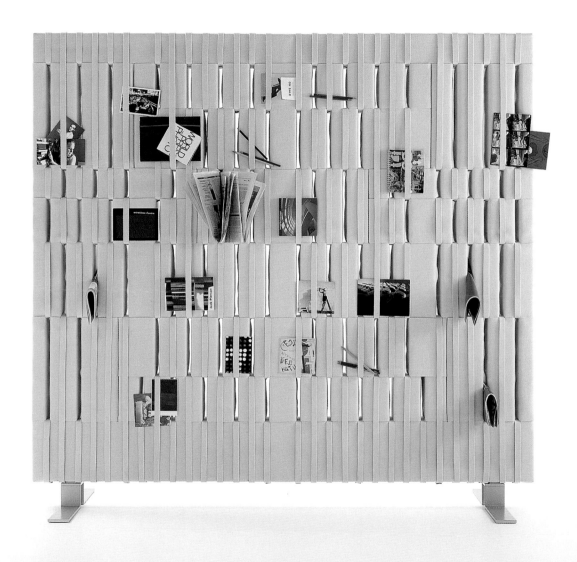

Between Lines

Materials Stainless steel, rubber
Dimensions 270 × 15 cm/
106¼ × 6 in.

||||||||||||||||||||||||||||||||||||||||||||||||||||||||||||||||

These rubber-coated letter bands can be
coiled up, unrolled and reshaped into any
configuration. Shanghai-based designers
Julie Mathias and Wolfgang Kaeppner
created the system as a triumph of
movement over stability, and to encourage
book lovers to read between the lines …
www.wokmedia.com

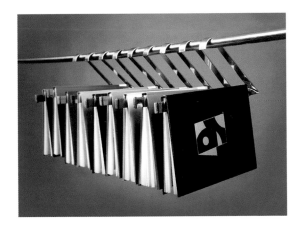

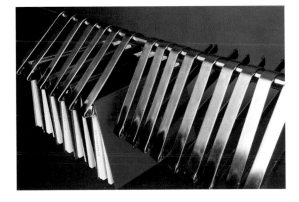

FA16
Material Nickel-plated brass
Dimensions 35 cm/
13¾ in. (diameter)
||||||||||||||||||||||||||||||||||||||||||||||||||||||||||||||||||||||||||||||||||||||||||||||||||||
A polished, rounded book-stand (not unlike a toast rack), useful
for storing thinner books and magazines. The FA16 was designed
by Fernando Akasaka from Brazil.
www.fakasaka.com

Hanger
Material Steel
Dimensions Various
||||||||||||||||||||||||||||||||||||||||||||||||||||||||||||||||||||||||||||||||||||||||||||||||||||
An idea that adapts the clothes hanger to suit books. Seoul
designer Wonsuk Cho's Hanger allows for the smart and original
storage of volumes, while also keeping a reader's place. The
Movement Bookcase (page 217) is by the same designer.
www.samulnoli.com

2

BIJOU BOOKSHELVES

A major problem facing book collectors is storage. While the designs presented in this book are ingenious, witty and colourful, some provide very limited space to shelve a substantial home library.

The restricted capacity of some shelves, however, can be a virtue. Those that offer little more than a ledge or cranny are perfect places to display much-loved volumes. They also present the chance for a statement to be made about the books they hold. Juxtaposed: Religion (page 254) was designed by Mike and Maaike, and produced as a limited edition of 50. It contains just seven books on one shelf – the texts of the world's most influential religions, sitting side by side. The customized manufacture means that all seven texts line up exactly. At a silent auction in November 2010, shelf 45, which was in almost perfect condition, was sold for US $5,525.

'A book on its own is very different from a book in the context of other books,' says designer Maaike Evers. 'Most families subscribe to one religion and therefore would own only one of these books. Religion can have the effect of segregation and causing a lack of understanding of other people. It seems especially timely today to encourage mutual understanding between faiths.'

Sometimes a large bookcase is also simply not practical. Historically, lighthouses located in remote areas had no access to services, and so supplies were generally delivered by tender ships. One item commonly found on board was a small library-box, filled with books and switched from station to station, supplying reading material to the lighthouse keepers and their families.

<<

Easy Reader

Materials Birch plywood
Dimensions 130 × 50 × 83 cm/
51¼ × 19¾ × 32¾ in.

||||||||||||||||||||||||||||||||||||||||||||||||||||||||||||||||||||||||||||||||||||||||||||||||||||||||

A streamlined version of Bookinist (page 158) by Nils Holger
Moormann, who says of it: 'Reading, sitting, loading, relaxing.
Quite simply.'

www.moormann.de

Pocket Library

Materials MDF, wood, castors, piano hinge, seat belts
Dimensions 65 × 55 × 55 cm/
25⅜ × 21⅝ × 21⅝ in.

||||||||||||||||||||||||||||||||||||||||||||||||||||||||||||||||||||||||||||||||||||||||||||||||||||||||

Ariel Jacubovich uses a system of adjustable belts to keep volumes
safe inside this luggage-like bookcase, which also features wheels
to make it more portable. It opens up like a puzzle to provide
ample shelf space.

www.arieljacubovich.com.ar

Book Hook

Materials Beech, birch, oak

Dimensions 12 × 10 × 17 cm/
4¾ × 4 × 6¾ in.

||||||||||||||||||||||||||||||||||||||||||||||||||||||||||||||||||||||||||||||||||||||||||||||

Tell Ritterbach's dislike of scrappy bookmarks led him to
design the Book Hook, which offers a convenient stand
on which to rest your book – keeping your place
without damaging the spine.

www.bookhook.de

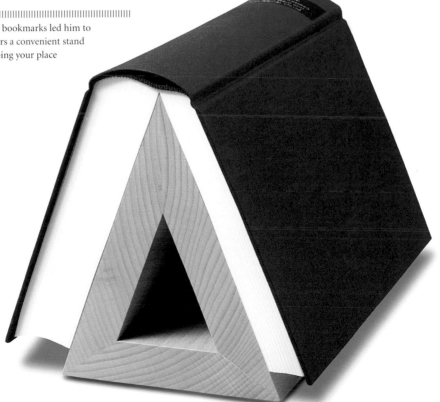

Book Box

Material Wood
Dimensions 35 × 35 × 47 cm/
13¾ × 13¾ × 18½ in.
||||||||||||||||||||||||||||||||||||||||||||||||||||||||||||||||||||||
Book Box is made out of factory-waste
wood collected in Denmark. Individual
units can be stacked on top of each other
or hung on the wall, while the built-in
shelves mean the boxes can be rotated
and used on their sides, with the legs
offering extra shelf space.
www.amyhunting.com

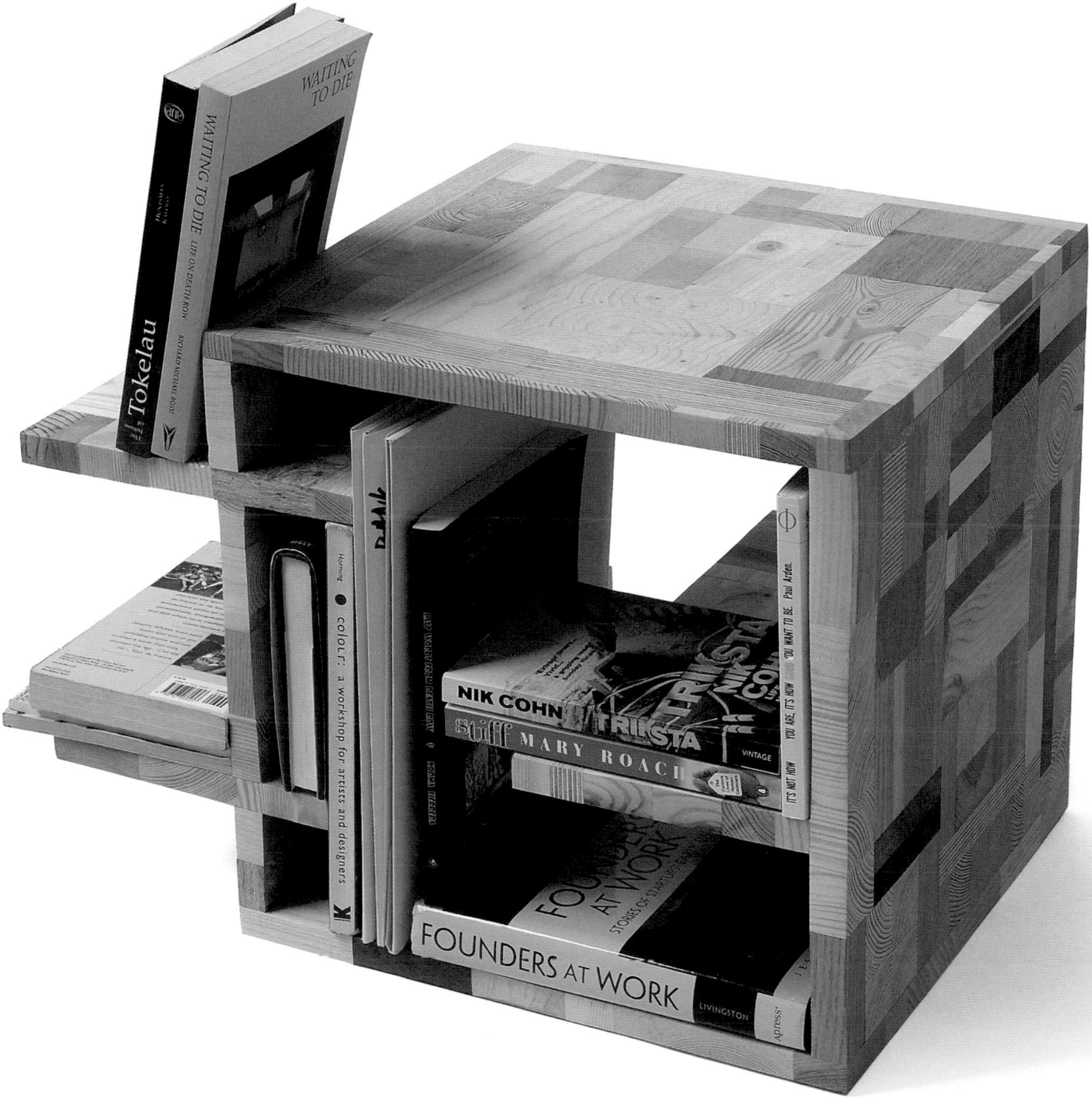

Bijou Bookshelves

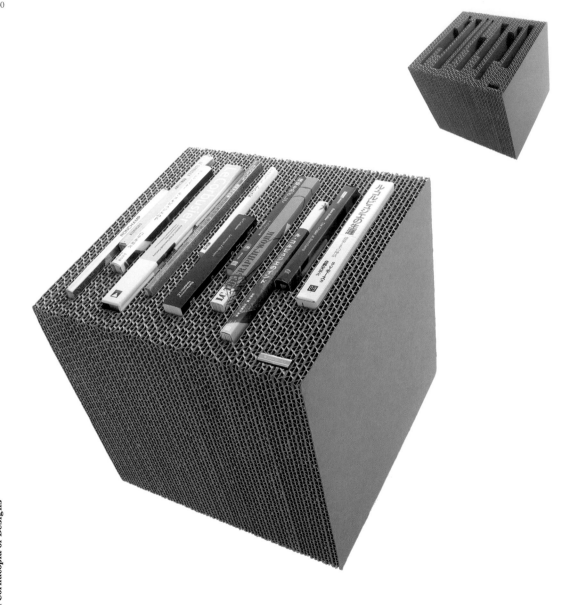

< Book and Shelf

Material Cardboard
Dimensions 36 × 36 × 36 cm/
14¼ × 14¼ × 14¼ in.
||||||||||||||||||||||||||||||||||||||||||||||||||||||||||||||||||||||||||||||||||||||||
Oki Sato built a shelf (cutting, assembling and gluing the layers)
to fit titles chosen by bookshop director Haba Yoshitaka. Behind
the metal plate featuring the brand name is a small pamphlet
containing information about the books in the shelf.
www.nendo.jp

Books-to-go

Materials Plastic laminated birch ply, stainless steel fittings,
skateboard wheels, vintage wallpaper
Dimensions 78 × 22 × 31 cm/
30¾ × 8¾ × 11⅛ in.
||||||||||||||||||||||||||||||||||||||||||||||||||||||||||||||||||||||||||||||||||||||||
Books-to-go is a mobile bookshelf to accompany readers on their
travels. The stackable shelving system includes a clamp and a set
of wheels: once you are ready to move off, simply tighten the
clamp to secure the books and then wheel away.
www.designbyrose.co.uk

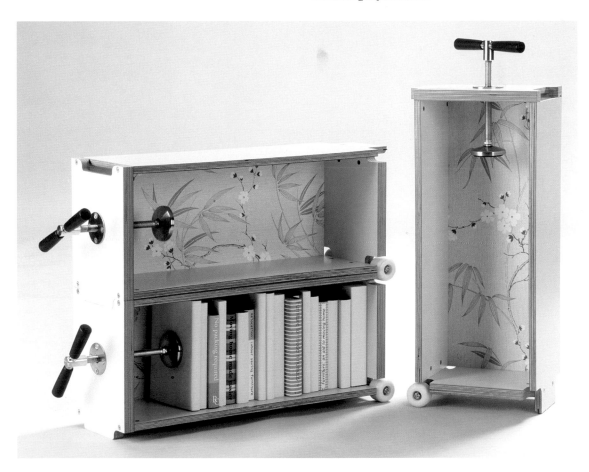

Bijou Bookshelves

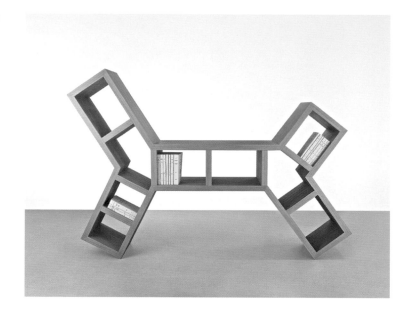

Reservoir Dog
Material Wood
Dimensions 190 × 32 × 130 cm/
74⅞ × 12⅝ × 51⅛ in.
||||||||||||||||||||||||||||||||||||||||||||||||||||||||||||||||||||
Inspired by the shape of a (reasonably
large) canine, Reservoir Dog from India
Mahdavi Furniture in Paris has nine
separate compartments for books.
www.indiamahdavi.com

Book Case
Material Suitcases
Dimensions Various
||||||||||||||||||||||||||||||||||||||||||||||||||||||||||||||||||||
A moveable, temporary public reading
room housed in a travelling suitcase
(sometimes two), perfect for transporting
quick reads, such as essays, short stories
and poetry. Designers Makeshift are
always looking to send their Book
Case to festivals, and the content varies
according to the event it's visiting.
Readers are encouraged to leave notes
for each other using correspondence cards
hidden in volumes. The Book Case can
be made to order, and appropriate book
donations are welcome.
www.makeshift.com.au

Ele

Materials Velcro, pine, cotton
bindings
Dimensions 75 × 9 × 90 cm/
29½ × 3⅜ × 35½ in.
||||||||||||||||||||||||||||||||||||||||||||||||||||||||||||||||||||||
A bookshelf made of six identical shapes
of machine-cut pine by Anaïs Calderón
from Lausanne, Switzerland. More pieces
can be added to form different
compositions. Ele can sit on the floor,
but may also be attached to the wall.
www.coroflot.com/anaiscalderon

Juxtaposed: Religion

Materials Reclaimed hardwood, books

Dimensions 91 × 20 × 12 cm/ 35⅞ × 7⅞ × 4¾ in.

||||||||||||||||||||||||||||||||||||||||||||||||||||||||||||||||||

The Juxtaposed: Religion bookshelf comes with seven of the world's most influential religious texts. Precisely cut indentations mean that the books in the collection are presented at exactly the same level, despite any differences in size.

www.mikeandmaaike.com

History >

Material ABS (plastic)

Dimensions 33 × 10 × 3 cm/ 13 × 4 × 1¼ in.

||||||||||||||||||||||||||||||||||||||||||||||||||||||||||||||||||

'The story behind the bookshelf may not be obvious,' says Houston industrial designer Mason Bonar. 'It is about direction, exactly what an arrow signifies. The colour represents that which is the middle ground between white and black, holy and unholy. The rough, unfinished look is us human beings … '

www.masonbonar.com

Eli Shelf

Materials Mahogany, coated steel
Dimensions 18 × 24 × 70 cm/
7 × 9½ × 27⅜ in.
||||||||||||||||||||||||||||||||||||||||||||||||||||||||||||||||||||||||||||||||||||||||||||||||
An evolutionary step beyond a simple pile of books, Eli is designed
to hold a number of titles that are being browsed before they are
returned to their place on the main bookshelf. A built-in handle
makes lighter loads easy to move around. Studio Ve also designed
the Newton shelf (page 140).
www.studiove.com

Pablo
Material Oak
Dimensions 28 × 13 × 40 cm/
11 × 5⅛ × 15¾ in.

||||||||||||||||||||||||||||||||||||||||||||||||||||||||||||||||||||||||||||||||||||||||||||||

A shelf in the guise of a picture frame, offering a rectangular
halo that surrounds your favourite titles. Designed and made
in Germany by Judith Hoefel and Andrea Grossfuss.
www.pling-collection.com

Plus One

Materials Maple or walnut veneer, steel tube, wool
Dimensions 35 × 25 × 35 cm/
13¾ × 9¾ × 13¾ in.

||||||||||||||||||||||||||||||||||||||||||||||||||||||||||||||||||||||||||||||||||||||||||||||||||||||||||

Plus One is a supplementary shelf that clips on to the edge
of a normal bookcase, thanks to a U-shaped tube. It provides
additional book-storage space, or can be used to highlight
a few particularly important titles. Plus One is designed
by Matthias Ries, who also created the Piegato One (page 80).
www.matthiasries.com

Book Sconce
Material Powder-coated steel
Dimensions 18 × 15 × 15 cm/
7 × 5⅞ × 5⅞ in.
||||||||||||||||||||||||||||||||||||||||||||||||||||||||
The Book Sconce shows off those
favourite books that can get lost in
the mayhem of more ample bookshelves.
The mounting cleat is carefully hidden
behind the displayed book.
www.irondesigncompany.com

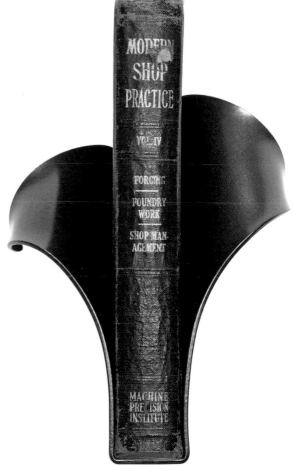

Book Porcupine

Materials MDF, high-gloss enamel
Dimensions 45 × 30 × 33 cm/
17¼ × 11¾ × 13 in.
||||||||||||||||||||||||||||||||||||||||||||||||||||||||||||||||||||||
There are 17 'shelves' of various sizes
in this bookcase, which is named after
the shape of its silhouette. Designer
Holly Palmer says the concept is
one of negative representation:
when a volume is taken away,
it leaves a fluorescent space behind it.
www.hollypalmeronline.co.uk

'Zjbtijbb'

Material Painted okoume hardwood ply
Dimensions 100 × 50 × 60 cm/
39⅜ × 19¾ × 23⅝ in.

||||||||||||||||||||||||||||||||||||||||||||||||||||||||||||||||||||||||||||||||||||||||||||||

According to Dutch designer Jurjen van Hulzen, 'zjbtijbb' stands
for 'zet-je-boek-terug-in-je-boekenkast-boekenkast' (translated:
'put-your-book-back-in-its-place-in-your-bookshelf-bookshelf').
He made it as a permanent reminder of the books he had bought
during a certain period.

www.jurjenvanhulzen.nl

Slim

Material Clear acrylic
Dimensions 16 × 7 × 140 cm/
6¼ × 2¾ × 55⅛ in.

|||||||||||||||||||||||||||||||||||||||||||||||||||||||||||||||||||||||||||||||||||||||||||||||||||||||||||||||||||||||||||

'Covers are made to be seen,' says Marianne van Ooij, whose restricted-size bookcase displays the fronts of books, almost like pictures in a frame. Each slot holds a couple of titles, making it easy to change what's on show.

www.mariannevanooij.com
www.slimshelving.com

Le Bouc

Materials MDF, varnished beech
Dimensions 55 × 40 × 50 cm/
21⅝ × 15¾ × 19¾ in.

||||||||||||||||||||||||||||||||||||||||||||||||||||||||||||||||||

Reminiscent of the Isokon Penguin
Donkey, Le Bouc is a portable, occasional
bookshelf with space on top to leave books
open at certain pages. Mathieu Gabiot's
design is available in red, black or white.
www.mathieu-g.be
www.lebouc.be

Lako
Material Steel wire
Dimensions 65 × 24 × 27 cm/
25⅝ × 9½ × 10⅝ in.
||||||||||||||||||||||||||||||||||||||||||||||||||||||||||||||||||||||||
A light and compact bent-steel rack
for storing books and magazines.
The handle at the apex makes it easy
to carry up to 20 titles around.
www.studiomacura.com

Laica

Material Lacquered fibreglass
Dimensions 120 × 33 × 36 cm/
47¼ × 13 × 14¼ in.
||||||||||||||||||||||||||||||||||||||||||||||||||||||||||||||
This minimalist floor rack, designed
by Francesco Innocenti for Zerogloss,
aims to impose balance on the bookshelf.
Zerogloss itself is a creative space for
design and art, based in a 1950s industrial
building in Vicenza, Italy.
www.zerogloss.it

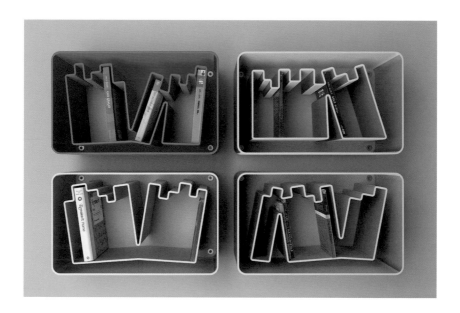

Bukan
Materials Powder-coated steel
Dimensions 55 × 55 × 16 cm/
21⅜ × 21⅜ × 6¼ in.
||||||||||||||||||||||||||||||||||||||||||||||||||||||||||||||||||||||
Charles Job has designed a small but handy
bookcase, with a bright typographical feel.
The Bukan is useful for storing both
magazines and large books.
www.charlesjob.com
www.mox.ch

< Book Storage
Material Injected plastic
Dimensions 55 × 20 × 30 cm/
21⅜ × 7⅞ × 11⅞ in.
||||||||||||||||||||||||||||||||||||||||||||||||||||||||||||||
Shahaf Levavi's Book Storage matches
a 1970s feel with a skyline aesthetic.
Books slot neatly into their individual
places, and additional units can be added
when necessary. Levavi is also the creator
of the Compushelf (page 173).
shahaf.levavi@gmail.com

Books and Essays

The Book on the Bookshelf, Henry Petroski (New York, 1999)

'Books as Furniture', Nicholson Baker, *New Yorker*, 12 June 1995. Collected in *The Size of Thoughts: Essays and Other Lumber* (London and New York, 1996)

Books Do Furnish a Room, Anthony Powell (London and Boston, 1971)

Books Do Furnish a Room, Leslie Geddes-Brown (London and New York, 2009)

On Books and the Housing of Them, William Ewart Gladstone (New York, 1898)

A Brief Illustrated History of the Bookshelf, Marshall Brooks (Delhi, NY, 1998)

The Care of Books: An Essay on the Development of Libraries and their Fittings, from the earliest times to the end of the Eighteenth Century, John Willis Clark (Cambridge, 1901)

A History of Reading, Alberto Manguel (New York, 1996)

At Home with Books: How Booklovers Live with and Care for Their Libraries, Estelle Ellis, Caroline Seebohm and Christopher Simon Sykes (New York, 1995)

< Falling Bookend

Material Metal
Dimensions 12 × 11 × 18 cm/
4¾ × 4⅜ × 7 in.
||||||||||||||||||||||||||||||||||||||||||||||||||||||||||||||||||||||||||||||||||||||||
The upright of the bookend is cleverly hidden inside the first book, which should ideally be a hardback. In this design a figure is seen attempting, unsuccessfully, to hold back an avalanche of books.
www.artori-design.com

House Beautiful: Decorating with Books, Marie Proeller Hueston (New York, 2006)

Libraries, Candida Höfer (London, 2006)

Library: An Unquiet History, Matthew Battles (New York, 2003)

The Library at Night, Alberto Manguel (New Haven, 2006)

Living With Books, Dominique Dupuich and Roland Beaufre (London and New York, 2010)

Living With Books, Alan Powers (New York, 1999)

Lunacy and the Arrangement of Books, Terry Belanger (New Castle, 1982)

The Most Beautiful Libraries in the World, Guillaume de Laubier and Jacques Bosser (London, 2003)

Phantoms on the Bookshelf, Jacques Bonnet (London, 2010)

Unpacking My Library: Architects and Their Books, Jo Steffens (New Haven, 2009)

Articles

'Boss Talk: John Makinson', *Wall Street Journal*, 9 May 2011

'Creative New Uses for Books', Rob Walker, *New York Times*, 6 August 2010

'A Little Suspense Travels a Long Way', David Colman, *New York Times*, 27 January 2008

'A Revolving Bookcase by Agostino Ramelli', Bert S. Hall, *Technology and Culture*, 11:3 (July 1970) 389–400

'Rooms that lose none of their shelf life', Sarah Lonsdale, *Daily Telegraph*, 15 April 2008

'Shelf Life', Virginia Heffernan, *New York Times*, 4 March 2010

'The "Five-foot Shelf" Reconsidered', Adam Kirsch, *Harvard Magazine*, November–December 2001

'To have and to hold', Matthew Reisz, *Times Higher Education*, 17 December 2009

'What's a Culture Snob to Do?', James Wolcott, *Vanity Fair*, August 2009

'What's the next chapter for bookshelves?', Kim Palmer, *Minneapolis Star Tribune*, 28 March 2011

'Will tablets force bookcases to go the way of the TV armoire?', Richard Mullins, *Tampa Tribune*, 9 June 2011

'Will the home library survive the surge of the e-book?', Alice-Azania Jarvis, *Independent*, 17 June 2011

Online articles

'Are Bookshelves the Latest Hotel Craze?', Hotel Chatter, 12 November 2008
www.hotelchatter.com/story/2008/11/4/111536/761/hotels/Are_Bookshelves_the_Latest_Hotel_Craze

'Bookshelf and Self', Scott McLemee, Inside Higher Ed, 27 February 2008
www.insidehighered.com/views/mclemee/mclemee104

'Bookshelf Etiquette' Jennifer Schuessler, *New York Times*, 21 March 2008
http://artsbeat.blogs.nytimes.com/2008/03/21/bookshelf-etiquette/

'Britain: A Bookworm Nation', Legal and General, February 2008
www.legalandgeneralmediacentre.com/Press-Releases/Britain-A-bookworm-nation-141.aspx

'Decorative Books: The End of Print', Steven Heller, The Design Observer, 26 September 2009
http://observatory.designobserver.com/entry.html?entry=5997

'The New Memory Theater', Nathan Schneider, The Smart Set, 19 November 2010
www.thesmartset.com/article/article11191001.aspx

'What does your bookcase say about you?' BBC News Magazine, September 2009
http://news.bbc.co.uk/1/hi/8264572.stm

Other online resources

There are numerous book-themed online sites that frequently post photographs of bookshelves and bookcases. As well as Bookshelf, Anthony Dever's Bookshelf Porn (bookshelves and nothing but!) is worth a daily look. Design sites that often feature bookshelf projects include MoCo Loco, Design Milk, Yanko Design, dezeen, designboom and Trend Hunter.

http://theblogonthebook shelf.blogspot.com
http://bookshelfporn.com
http://mocoloco.com
http://design-milk.com
www.yankodesign.com
www.dezeen.com
www.designboom.com
www.trendhunter.com

For regular updates on all things bookshelf, join Alex on Facebook (www.facebook.com/bookshelvesbook).

ILLUSTRATION CREDITS

All illustrations are provided courtesy of the designer/designer-maker or manufacturer, with specific credits noted below:

19 **Library**, Jeppe Gudmundsen Holmgreen; 30 Playtime, Collin Hotermans; 31 Bookspile, Amberstudio; 38 **Chaos Theory**, Rolf Lang; 38 **FKY**, Vanja Solin; 44 **Pogo Library**, David Scheu; 46 **Ladder No. 1**, Kristof Vrancken; 57 **Weave**, Satoshi Asakawa; 64 **Collect Shelf**, Normann Copenhagen; 70 **Kaos**, Joachim Haslinger; 73 **Factor**, © Daniele Ansidei and JODR; 76 **Tensor Voting**, Elisa van der Linden; 84 **6 Degrees**, Janek Lutyk; 90–1 **Upside Down**, Aurélien Mole; 93 **Equilibrium**, Monica Barreneche; 132 **Roches**, Tahon & Bouroullec; 133 **Quattro Line**, Matthew Donaldson; 154 **Powerlight**, Ethan Kaplan and Leger Wanaselja Architecture; 157 **Nook,** Brad Knilans; 158 **Bookinist**, Jäger & Jäger; 184 **Cable Car Book Cart**, Shawn P. Calhoun; 202 **Bookshelf Dress**, Courtesy of Zero + Maria Cornejo; 208–9 **Bibliotheque Outlandia**, London Fieldworks; 212 **Sherman Contemporary Art Foundation Bibliotheca**, Peter Murphy, Chris Bosse, David Simmonds; 254 **Juxtaposed: Religion**, Mike and Maaike

ACKNOWLEDGMENTS

This book has been in development for several years, growing out of the Bookshelf blog, found at http://theblogonthebookshelf.blogspot.com. Along the way it has received fine support from many readers who have contributed ideas and comments, in particular Chris Routledge, Sarah Salway, Françoise Murat, Andrew Wilcox and Colin Shelbourn. The staff at Thames & Hudson were generous and supportive from the start of the project.

I have not designed a single one of the bookshelves or bookcases in these pages – the book is rather a testament to the amazing skill and creativity of the designers featured, who have been so generous with their help and advice. As Montaigne (himself the owner of some lovely curved bookshelves) wrote, 'I have gathered a garland of other men's flowers, and nothing is mine but the cord that binds them'.

ABOUT THE AUTHOR

Alex Johnson is a professional blogger and journalist. As well as curating the Bookshelf blog (http://theblogonthebookshelf.blogspot.com) he is part of the online team at the *Independent* newspaper, works as an editorial consultant for several charities and runs the Shedworking website (www.shedworking.co.uk) for homeworkers with garden offices. He lives in St Albans with his wife, three children and an ever-expanding collection of bookshelves.